Searching for a Man of Iron

"A very different sports book—not just about athletics, but about a powerful personal tale of a parent's and child's love that became apparent through a quest to do an Ironman. Every triathlete should read this. It's a book about athletics, nature, family connections, and healing."—**Bill Rogers**, Four-time winner of the New York City and Boston marathons

"I admire Martha Childs for having the will and discipline to finish the Ironman race. I also respect her for writing this stunning story—prose rich with her father's legacy."—**Iris Lee Underwood**, Author and poet

"An engaging and beautiful story about life, love, and achieving goals. I was touched, both as an Ironman competitor and a father, by how the love and respect for a parent could help someone accomplish one of the most fulfilling events in life: completing an Ironman competition."—**Joe Morton**, XanGo founder and six-time Ironman finisher

"A heartwarming, inspirational and motivating story that everyone can relate to. Having participated in several Ironmans myself, I found that this book dives deeply into the emotional psyche of what motivates us as humans, and inspires the hidden feelings that arise on that magical race day. I recommend this fascinating read to athletes of all ages, to understand the motivating drive behind an Ironman event. Excellent."—**Dr. Russell Craig,** Seven-time Ironman finisher

"Martha takes us on a vivid journey of two searching hearts. Her father-daughter saga connects two centuries, four generations, and a compelling episode of athletic endurance and accomplishment. Jump into this story. It will bring out the best in you."—**Christopher M. Clark**, Ph.D., Professor Emeritus, Michigan State University

Searching for a Man of Iron
©2012 by Martha Aubrey Cole

Cover art by Martha Aubrey Cole
Book and cover design by Fountain Publishing
Printed by Fidlar Doubleday

For more information or to order more copies
contact the author at 248-515-0778

ISBN 10: 1936665093
ISBN 13: 978-1-936665-09-9

SEARCHING FOR A
Man of Iron

Sue,
great meeting
you! I see
you as some one
crazy enough to consider
this!
Enjoy the journey
Martha

MARTHA AUBREY COLE

Designed by
FOUNTAIN PUBLISHING®

Foreword

How many children have had a parent or someone they dearly love die when they were young, and have spent the rest of their lives wondering what that loved one was really like? How many of these children have thought about researching their parent's life to find out more about them? And how many of these children have said, "I'm going to write a book about the parent I never knew"?

There are too many to count, and yet Martha Childs has actually done it. She has written a book about the dad she lost at the age of 11 in 1965.

In Martha's case the difficult problem of researching her father's life was made a bit easier. Her dad, Dandridge Cole, was a prominent personality during the Space Race of the late 1950's and the 1960's. His books, papers, broadcasts, presentations and speeches made him a person of great interest to write about and to remember. Today he is still considered one of the most futuristic thinkers who ever lived.

However, even with good resource material, writing is never easy, and glimmers of memories are often hard to pin down. Martha has worked hard, plodding along, exploring not only her dad's life but also her own short time with her dad.

You will be enchanted by what Martha has found, and by how she has intertwined her and her father's lives through patches and glimmers. Her easy writing style will pull you in. She lets us explore and feel with her. As large as the task may have seemed at times, Martha shows "her stuff" and brings her Ironman to the pages for all of us to experience along with her. This is a book of encouragement that says, "Don't be afraid. Jump!"

Roy Scarfo
Dan Cole's good friend and Space Artist for
Beyond Tomorrow by Dan Cole

Introduction

*Man is harder than iron, stronger than stone
and more fragile than a rose.*
—Turkish Proverb

For the last five years, I have wanted to write a book about the man who gave me life. I have done a lot of research into who this person was. Just Google his name, Dandridge M. Cole, and you get numerous web listings. But I wanted more.

My dad died when I was eleven, and I lost a big part of my world, a big part of who I am. Perhaps because it was easier and less painful, I pretty much went on as if he hadn't existed. I stopped asking questions for fear I'd stir up old hurt, so Daddy disappeared in a bigger way than just his physical absence.

After years of searching and discovering, I set about to record the information I had learned about my dad, but I needed a spark to give life to all the data I'd gathered.

In time, the right vehicle presented itself—my story of the Ironman race I completed in 2000. From what I had learned about my dad, I realized that he was the inspiration for taking that challenge. He was the reason I was drawn to it. So I used my fourteen-hour race as a means to present his story.

When I told my aunt Aubrey (my dad's sister) my plan, she said, "That's a wonderful idea! Do you know what your father's favorite book was when he was growing up?"

"No,"I answered thinking how little I really knew about my dad.

"**Men of Iron**, by Howard Pyle", she told me. When I heard this, I knew I had to go with this idea. Voices in my mind as well as voices from my family and friends asked me, "What makes you think you can write a book? You don't know anything about writing a book!"

Fortunately, another voice in my head also asked, "What made you think you could do an Ironman?"

It was probably the same voice that told me I could get a book published when I was nine years old.

He was working in his study on his book, **Beyond Tomorrow**, and I brought in a little book I'd written called, **Scary Stories**. I asked him if he thought I could get it published.

Daddy carefully held my treasure, looking through my feeble attempt at writing. He could have told me the truth, that there was no way that book would have been published. Instead, he said, "Of course you can. You can do whatever you set out to do." I certainly didn't realize what a strong message that was when he said it. I ignored it and even forgot about it over the years.

But that message came back to me when I started thinking about the possibility of doing an Ironman. It was also that clear, strong voice that told me I could write this book, and that the Ironman race was just a step in the process to get to this point.

So I set out to write about "one of America's outstanding visionaries of science." (Fortune Magazine, 1964). Dad's accomplishments and achievements were great, but my story turned out to be more about the father—the strong, yet tender-loving parent that instilled in his children the values of creativity, the courage to dream and to strive toward goals some might think inconceivable, and to appreciate this universe God has given us.

It's been an interesting adventure, just as the training and

the race were. I've relived the race in a fuller and more profound way than I ever could have imagined.

I did the Ironman almost eleven years ago, but when I
started writing about it, the details came back with such clarity,
perhaps even clearer than at the time I was doing it. At the
time, I was so engrossed in the physical aspects that I didn't
realize the depth of what I was doing. There were points in the
race when I became so exhausted it was almost as if my spirit
left my body and was watching from the sidelines, encouraging
me along.

And just as the race details came back more vividly, so
also did the details of my childhood—even more so. Those
years lost in the throes of grief came back as if I was there again
visiting my past.

Men of Iron...the story of the amazing adventures of a
young son of a lord unjustly accused of treason, back in the
days of chivalry in England during the reign of Henry IV.

I think of the young boy, Miles Falworth, and of the rise
from his service under a powerful lord to knighthood. Then I
think of another young boy in the late 1920's and early 1930's,
Danny Cole, whose imagination was stirred by such adventures, the boy who would go on to become an adventurer into
the world beyond this planet. I have a deep feeling of gratitude
that I was honored to have such a man as a father.

I've allowed my father to come back into my life now, not
fearing the pain and ache that the memories have stirred any
longer. I've learned to embrace them. It is that ache that allows
him to live on in my heart.

My dad was a man unafraid to step out beyond the con-
fines of conventional thought, a man of integrity and honor...a
man of iron.

Chapter One:
The Swim

*"Space is a sea without end which washes on
countless strange and exotic shores; where the
conceivable forms of the living and the dead
are greatly outnumbered by the inconceivable;
where the known is lost in the unknown;
where new dangers hide in undiscovered shadows
in unimagined forms; where new goals can
challenge and new beauty and wonder can
inspire the spirits of all people...for all time."*
—Dandridge MacFarlan Cole and Donald W. Cox,
Islands in Space

I would've laughed and thought you ridiculous if you had told me years ago that I'd be standing here on this beach in Panama City, Florida on this particular November day. Here with the salty water lapping at my feet, the smell of the sea fills my head, overwhelming me as questions rise up in a tidal wave of doubt.

My toes sink into the sand, and at once I am transported to a time when I was three. I was standing on a diving board with my toes curling tightly over the edge and my eyes pointed downward into a vast pool of blue. I felt so small, so full of fear (not unlike my current emotions!) but saw my dad with his arms held out, encouraging me to jump. And even now I can hear his strong reassuring words, "Don't be afraid."

A seagull flies past with its laughing voice and jolts me back to where I am.

Just yesterday I was looking at this long, white beach with vacationers speckling the pure landscape, relaxing and enjoying the warmth of the sun. What a haven of peace and tranquility. It seemed fit for a postcard to send home.

But not today! It's 7:00 a.m. and I'm standing at the water's edge surrounded by some 2,000 other wetsuit-clad bodies, and I've never felt such fear for my life. I look ahead to my right. There's a cordoned-off corral with the pink, yellow, and white-capped elite athletes sans wetsuits. There are different rules for the athletes, different temperatures where wetsuits are allowed or not: 72 degrees or colder for the elite (the professionals) and 75 degrees or under for the age-groupers. I'm ever so thankful that we age-groupers were allowed our wetsuits today, and I take great comfort in knowing that at least I will float when I get knocked out.

Up ahead, the elites anxiously await their opportunity to win and break through the tape, while I look side to side at those of us just hoping to survive long enough to finish.

To my left I see the athletes stretching almost a quarter mile down the beach—that littoral zone filled with anxiety. I wonder if my friends are somewhere down there. I look behind, and for as far as I can see it's just men, big guys in neon green swim caps. Usually, I feel a sense of comfort with the male companions I train with and enjoy the bond and symbiotic connection. But now they terrify me. Where are all the women? I see none of the light blue caps around me. They obviously had more sense than I did and are further toward the back of this mass of people. What have I done? I am going to be crushed! I feel like a lemming, waiting to follow the others off the cliff to our death. I envision crossing myself and I'm not even Catholic.

My heart races, pounding right through my neck into my ears. I am flushed with the sense of impending doom. Thankfully I ate breakfast many hours ago when I woke at the ungodly hour of 4:00am. (Woke!? Who sleeps on a night like this?) So hopefully I am in no danger of losing my meal here.

In all those years of watching the Hawaii Ironman on TV back in the mid 80's and 90's, I never imagined then that I would be one of these 2000 "few" about to embark on what was to be one of the greatest life changing events I could experience.

There's a certain look to the face of an athlete about to embark on a journey such as this. I saw it in the faces when I arrived at the transition area two hours ago, everyone walking around so dazed. I imagine it's similar to cattle going off to slaughter, or even young men going off to war—a blank stare of gravitas; a mixture of questioning the present while also looking toward the future, the goal, the end.

A fellow athlete I trained with two days earlier told me to place myself at the very front of the pack if I hoped to get an hour time for the 2.4 mile Ironman swim. But now I worry that this was a mistake. What was I thinking? I'm just a tiny, fragile, 112 pound fool! Never a "front of the class" type, you'd always find me hiding at the back. And I've never attempted anything of this magnitude before. Sure, I've done sprint distance triathlons with their half-mile swims, and even the Olympic distance with the one-mile swim. But I've never gone into the water with this many people all at once to do this kind of mileage.

I take a step further into the brine, hoping that the salt will preserve this moment for just a bit longer. But do I really want to prolong this agony? It's true what they say about triathletes being masochists by nature. A chill runs down my spine though it's a warm, 60 degree morning.

The hazy, red sunrise draws my attention to my left. The powerful big ball of fire inspires ideas of rebirth and baptism. I think back to my beginnings.

Once again my thoughts turn to that person who instilled the sense of adventure in me, and the belief that I could do anything I set my mind to—a man who encouraged me to be-lieve in myself. And with that strength from him I inherited the drive to do the extraordinary, to reach for the stars, to dream and to dream big. Yes, I can throw all the blame on him! It's because of him I'm in this mess right now!

Dandridge MacFarlan Cole, a man considered one of the most stimulating and thought-provoking geniuses of the space age, was my beginning.

The list of accomplishments in his short lifetime is a long one. In college he was a gymnast, diver, and medical student, and he spent his army days as a paratrooper, lifeguard, ju jitsu instructor, and poet. Later he'd be lauded as a teacher, scientist, physicist, inventor, writer, radio commentator, and aerospace engineer, written up in articles from magazines such as *Time*, *Fortune*, *Omni*, *Ad Astra*, *New York Mirror*, and *Science Digest*, and even mentioned in a Star Trek novel, **The Romulan Prize**.

He graduated from Princeton University with a B.S. in

chemistry in 1943, followed by a year at the Columbia University College of Physicians and Surgeons. He received a Master's Degree in Physics from the University of Pennsylvania in 1949. But along with these many impressive hats he wore, perhaps his greatest achievement was that he was a loving son, brother, husband, and father to six kids.

The years peel back to a time long ago in Colorado when Daddy taught me how to swim, and more importantly, to love the water.

The images come flooding back of my father guiding us to put our faces in the tub or bathroom sink just to get the feel of the water, to become comfortable with it. He guided me along with my brothers and sisters as if we were a team. He was every bit the team leader.

In recent years, reading the letters he wrote to his sister and mother while in boot camp back in the early 1940's, I found stories of him teaching many of the servicemen to swim. He was responsible for teaching hundreds of men of all ranks who had come totally unprepared for the rigors of boot camp. In a letter from May 1943 he wrote:

"I seem to have a racket in the swimming business. Starting Monday we teach the 297th to swim. About 200 of them don't know anything about it, can't even stay afloat ...quite a job to take them all the way from beginners, to swimmers capable of swimming underwater thru burning oil, with clothes and full packs on, etc."

But later on in the letter he referred to this as, "lots of fun and very pleasant."

Quite often Daddy was given responsibilities usually delegated to officers, but he was just a private in the Army. He had wanted to be in the paratroopers, so he gave up a commission he earned by going through medical school at Columbia. He could have been an officer with the navy, but the lure of jumping out of planes appealed to him more.

He was definitely in charge when it came to his family. Dad was a bit of a neat freak, and he ran our home like a little military base, with inspections and even marching. And sometimes he'd line us up for punishment when we needed it. I never felt fear in those times of penalizing. I knew he didn't enjoy this punitive aspect of parenting. Perhaps he just needed to feel a presence of order. How do months in boot camp and fighting in Europe shape a person? How does it change them? What kind of imprint does it leave?

I'll never forget one night when we were living in Bryn Athyn, Pennsylvania. I must have been about eight or nine. My brothers, sisters, and I were rounded up for a group punishment. We all gathered in the living room and lined up behind the long wooden table in front of the couch.

It was a fine piece of furniture—darkly stained, thick wood with black wrought-iron securing the legs, very functional for a big family. My dad had carefully and lovingly crafted this slab of wood with his own two hands, even down to the details of cutting the corners and sanding them down to protect us from harm. So it struck me as a little contradictory to be leaning over this particular piece of furniture to be paddled. Perhaps it was a way to show us he still cared, even with the imminent discipline about to befall us.

But this night was different. I cleverly tried to outwit my dad by putting a Golden book in my pants to shield my poor bottom. His reaction has stayed with me more vividly than any of the actual punishments ever could. He burst into laughter and was unable to follow through with his plan. And perhaps that is why, to this day, I haven't any bad feelings about being punished.

Thoughts of the community pool in Littleton, Colorado come to mind, and once again I am up there in my pink cotton bathing suit with the ruffles on my butt, on that diving board looking down to the water. I laugh, picturing the silly rubber swim caps we wore with the snap strap under the chin. (We surely have come a long way with those!) I still remember the smell of that rubber. Even the enticing waft of chlorine rising up from the blue couldn't dispel my feeling so isolated and alone. On the deck, oblivious to my fear, people milled about engrossed in their enjoyment of the beautiful, clear summer day.

With my arms held closely to my chest and shivers shaking my tiny frame, I looked down and there he was—my great protector. He was so strong, so confident in my abilities. I couldn't let him down. I jumped. Every time he asked, with his squinting smile and playful patting on the water, I jumped.

It comes back to me, and for a moment a smile relaxes my face. My fears calm ...

And then the gun goes off!

I splash tumultuously into the water. There are arms and legs everywhere, creating a wild, raging, savage feel to what is usually a serene catharsis. Other days swimming is a meditative, peaceful respite from the everyday distractions of my life. It is a time to reflect, or just be in the moment, allowing me to focus on my breathing, to flow, to stretch, to feel at one with the soothing fluid. Whatever traumas going on at the time are washed away in the embryonic world of water. All is well.

But not here, not today. This is like nothing I have ever experienced before. The calm water has turned into a churning, frothing, agitated frenzy like the spawning of salmon—a fight upstream against peers with one common goal.

The Ironman swim is like getting dropped into a blender. You are punched, kicked, scratched, and pushed under. I can picture my face smashed up against the edge of the glass container, wide-eyed and terrified. It truly is a fight for survival. A friend suggested I grow my nails for the event! Another friend called it MMA—mixed martial arts—just add water!

I swim as if my life depends on it. I know I can't stop, for even just a moment, not to catch my breath or adjust my goggles, or get my sighting in. Forget looking for the big, orange, triangular-shaped buoys that line the course, even though I'd so carefully trained myself to breathe on either side so I could find them.

I struggle through a mile with only a primitive, survivalistic response driving me. It's a "being in the moment" experience. I keep my wits about me, telling myself to just keep swimming, swimming with all my strength. Whatever I do, DON'T STOP! I read not long ago that one should learn to put their goggles back on while in the process of swimming. Now I know why.

I feel a kick here, a punch there. I'm being pummeled all along the way. I catch a glimpse of the face on the guy that batters me, and I search his eyes to find some glimmer of human kindness. But all I find is that shark-like stare, a primordial glare of single purpose.

Suddenly, I get a kick in the face hard enough to feel as though my goggles are now imbedded into my face. The pain leaves me a little dazed, but I have to brush it off and keep going. I can't help wondering if this is not like a battle in war. I picture soldiers getting wounded, continuing on, shaking it off. Oh, blessed adrenaline, with your "fight or flight" surge, protect me the rest of my way!

After the first mile and a quarter we come out of the water, run down the beach a bit past a table covered with green cups of Gatorade (does anyone really stop for that?) and then back into the water for another mile-plus swim. I can't imagine drinking any Gatorade. I've already drunk enough salt water to last me a lifetime. Who needs electrolytes? I also swallowed a mouthful of gasoline from the boats for added fuel. But at least it's not "burning oil!" There are a number of boats, kayaks, and people on surf boards lining the course to watch us, and to keep us safe.

In some Ironman races, I've seen scuba divers in the water keeping a watchful eye, or sometimes filming the underwater activity. I think of the pictures I've seen in magazines, or the shots on TV from underneath, looking up at the dark silhouettes—bodies in motion, reminding me of those shots of the seals in nature programs. And always, always lurking in the background is that shadowy figure of a shark. Surely, no shark would brave the waters surrounding this mass of neoprene bodies.

Only a week or two ago, I was listening to Paul Harvey on the radio saying that they have found that sharks will not attack animals that have been struck by lightning. Immediately upon hearing this, I raised my fist and exclaimed, "Yes!" thinking back to the two times I was struck by lightning when younger. Finally, something that had created such terror in the past was providing comfort. But then again the voice of reason questioned, "How in the world can they really test this theory?" Despite the voice of reason, I choose to take comfort in this information all the same.

Now that the "school" of swimmers has thinned, my movements are smoother. I feel like I am swimming rather than battling for survival. I stretch my strokes out, reaching and pulling, the fear now fading behind me in the vast green of the Gulf.

It's at moments like these, when it becomes so relaxed and easy, that it's as if I were swimming through creme brulee, not that creme brulee would be easy to swim through, it's just that I love it that much!

Awareness of the depth of the water, which went unnoticed during the first loop, now hits me with full force. We swim out a half mile into this enormous body of water, and the immensity makes me feel so insignificant. I see a dome-shaped jellyfish floating along with a tiny school of fish circling it. I'm a little child again, watching my dad do handstands on the bars of the pool ladders of any pool we ever visited.

Dad was a member of the Princeton diving team, and I have numerous mental images of him doing handstands, flips, pikes, twists and half-twists off any diving board he was around. That thin plank of fiberglass always pulled him like a magnet. He was also on the gymnastics team in his college days back in the early 40's. I didn't know this until much later in my life, long after he was gone, so I never got to ask him about it. I would have liked to know what he loved about diving and gymnastics, why he chose the rings and the high bar. Could he do the iron cross? I can imagine him in that pose, so strong, so calm, so confident. Oh, to be able to know what went through his head while competing. What were the tricks he used? What was his "style"? What was the bond like between him and his teammates?

It's funny, back in my high school days at the Academy

Girls School in Bryn Athyn (where athletic competing was looked upon as unladylike), we did do a semester of gymnastics, and I remember loving that class. Now after all these years I have a new understanding of why I loved it. It was inborn! It's amazing what interesting paths we tend to take without knowing why. In retrospect we can see the inclinations stemming from an obvious source.

When I was ten, my dad talked me into taking diving lessons at the community pool in Bryn Athyn. It was a beautiful, but not grandiose, outdoor facility, situated behind the elementary school, and next to the high school football field. That pool was a great meeting place in the summer for all in the community, young and old.

I remember not wanting to take the diving lessons, but doing it all the same—probably for that perennial need to please, and how humiliating an experience that first dive off the high board was. Not having been cautioned that it's not a good idea to dive in a two-piece bathing suit, I learned the hard way, and ended up with the bottom of my suit around my knees! I wore a tee shirt over my suit thereafter, as I was never fond of a one piece bathing suit.

Having had my father die when I was eleven, I lost out on a lot of the obvious "why's" behind my proclivity toward certain things. It's only in recent years, through research into who he was, that I have discovered numerous answers as to who I am. Even today I'm struck with the coincidence from another boot camp letter he wrote about "talk of a three-day trip for the lifeguards to Panama City," when he was at Camp Rucker in Alabama teaching the servicemen to swim. How odd for me to end up here, possibly on the same beach 57 years later. Such a fitting connection!

*****

I have an old black and white photo of my dad, his brother, and his sister as children hand in hand on the beach at Lake Erie. They stand as faded silhouettes against a brilliant sunny background. When I look at the photo, I can almost hear the laughter as they play. I wonder what life would've been like back then. I feel a twinge of envy thinking of how much less chaotic their world seemed. My father was born in Sandusky, Ohio on February 19, 1921, third son to Robert Macfarlan Cole III and Wertha Pendleton Cole. William (Bill), Dad's older brother had a twin (James) who died shortly after birth. There was a younger sister Aubrey (whom I inherited my middle name from), and then Robert (Bobby) some years younger. They lived in a two-story white house on 42nd Street, not far from Lake Erie. That's where "Danny" learned to swim.

My dad loved walking on his hands in the water. He was a gymnast from the very beginning, a skinny, active boy with his deep brown eyes and wavy brown hair, forever on the move. He loved the outdoors, but even when he was stuck inside he'd be setting up cushions in the living room to do flips and cartwheels into.

And if he wasn't moving, he was creating. He had a collection of rockets he'd carved out of balsa wood. They hung from his ceiling, filling his room with the wonders of space.

From very early on Dad had dreams of becoming Buck Rogers. Though he never became the spaceman he'd dreamed of being, he went on to do great things for the Space program in the late '50s and early '60s. Even as an adult his dreams never waned. His imagination led him to design not just rockets for NASA, but all sorts of conceptualized space habitats including hollowed out asteroids and even some underwater habitats.

As I swim through the salty water, I picture the painting in **Beyond Tomorrow**, his third and last book. The illustration, by my father's good friend and collaborator, Roy Scarfo, (they were known as the 'odd couple' at G.E) is my father's idea of an underwater laboratory. The caption reads "an early step toward Macro Life." Further along in the text comes a prophetical statement: "Our current efforts to communicate with the 'intelligent' porpoise may be just a dress rehearsal for our future attempts to talk to extraterrestrial beings." I imagine myself as one of the people riding on a dolphin around the cylindrical-shaped living area, and wonder if indeed we will someday talk to extraterrestrials, or perhaps, already have!

I think about the connection between space and water, the subtle, yet strong pull of gravity affecting both our tides and our thoughts. Both are largely unexplored frontiers.

My father's ideas were limitless and always exceeded the barriers of conservative thought. His visions and dreams were as open as the universe.

Back in the mid 1980's, after my grandfather Cole's passing, I inherited my grandmother's astronomy book collection. These books, dating from the late 1800's to the early 1900's, are wonderful examples of astronomy. They express the beautiful language and the timelessness of space. In one such book, **Astronomy With an Opera Glass** (published in 1888), I found passages describing the wonders that my father was so enchanted by. "It is a plain road from the earth to the stars, though mortal feet cannot tread it."

Sometimes I wonder if my father's feet were the feet of a mortal. If you listen to some of the legends and stories about him, you'd be wondering the same. At 39 years of age he was likened to a modern day Leonardo Da Vinci in a *Fortune Magazine* article. He was dubbed "The Way Out Man" in an ABC documentary and a magazine article, and was listed as a futurologist and visionary. His feet may have been mortal, but they were rarely touching the ground. I often pictured him having feet like the god Mercury, with little wings attached at the heels.

*****

Almost 80 years after my father's birth, 35 years after his death, I would do a two-mile swim competition outside of Cleveland in Lake Erie, not far from the place he learned to swim. I wish I had known this at the time. It would have meant a lot more knowing he began his early love of water in that lake.

Swimming has always been a connection that linked me to this man, a connection that threads deeply into the fibers of my spirit. While some people may dream of being able to fly, often my dreams consist of being able to stay underwater for long periods of time without worrying about having to breathe.

I remember a time when I held onto a pool ladder under water to keep my air-filled body from floating up to the surface. I was playing a game with a friend to see how long we could stay under. I stayed down for three of his breaths and was beginning to think as he bobbed up and down that maybe I could just stay under indefinitely. Water seems to have the ability to cross over that Time-Space barrier for me. Seconds slip into a realm where time stops, and are gently held by the tenuous yet powerful grip of a liquid world. But then again, it may have just been the lack of oxygen getting to my brain. Did my father also share these dreams? Apparently he must have, as he invented and designed frogmen equipment at one point while in the military. I heard a story, and then read of it in one of his boot camp letters. O.S.S (Office of Strategic Services) agents had come to check him out because they thought he'd stolen the idea of the underwater breathing apparatus that had just been developed within the government. Often, the same ideas are created at the same time by one or more individuals. It's as if these ideas float around in the universe until one or more minds pick them out of the ether.

Yes, I was raised to love the water. When we moved from Colorado to Pennsylvania, it wasn't long before my father found us a home with an inground pool. He would say, "A pool is not a luxury. It is a necessity." And though he died not long after moving there, we would all go on to swim and play in that pool for endless summer days. I felt a great sense of sadness that he hadn't been able to enjoy the pool he so carefully found for us. But for many years, after he was gone, I felt his presence in that water, like Poseidon, or perhaps a gentler, more amiable version of "The Creature from the Black Lagoon", a character my dad had enjoyed.

My reverie reminds me of times I watched my dad with that darn nose clip that was always hanging around his neck or clenched to his nose. I thought it looked silly, but now I understand his desire to extend those underwater moments without having water filling your sinuses with a "headrush." He would swim lengths of a pool submerged, always trying to see how far he could go with just one breath.

My aunt has told me numerous times that they used to call him 110% Dan, always giving more than expected, always going above and beyond. It could be my imagination, but I seem to recall he could do two full lengths of our large backyard pool in one breath.

Heroes will come and go, but none are so poignant and unforgettable as the ones in the shape of our parent.

*****

From 1960, when we first moved from Colorado to the Philadelphia area, we would vacation every summer at the seashore, or Lake Wallenpaupak in the Pocono Mountains. Vacationing near some large body of water was mandatory.

My dad loved the ocean. He bought a surf board at a Ron Jon Surf shop in New Jersey and spent time mastering the art, once again probably inspired by his gymnastic abilities. Little did I realize at the time how "cool" he was. He was a part of the surfing culture that suddenly became the rage in the early 60's. I'll never forget the surfing competition we watched. Well, maybe I don't remember the competition so much as how I got my tee shirt signed by a pro surfer, Harold "Iggy" Ige. I begged my mom not to wash that shirt for months after. Not having permanent markers was a real drawback to autograph collecting in those days! But the pictures I have of my dad running out of the surf with his board tucked under his muscular arm will remain marked in my memory like no permanent marker could ever capture.

And of course, Daddy somehow talked me into going out on that surf board, though I never did ride a wave in. Images of just sitting on that board out beyond the breakers fill me with the sure sense of security I felt rocking there. There we were in that calm zone past the wild waves, my father's strong hand on that newly-waxed island of fiberglass, holding me steady. It fed my constant desire to be singled out of the crowd that we called family. He was good at that, taking time with each one of us, making us feel special and appreciated.

Every time I now travel to the sea—whichever coast it is, the Atlantic, Pacific, or Gulf—I can hardly wait to open the windows to smell that sea fragrance. The odor of salt water and seaweed stirs in me such childhood longings that I can barely contain myself. It takes me back to a time when life was easy, when one had little to worry about. The deep blue skies, the grass-covered sand dunes with the soft, warm wind blowing across them, baby toads we'd find hopping here and there among the razor-sharp green blades—all this will stay with me forever etched in the recesses of memory, hidden, then awakened suddenly by some picture or aroma.

*****

My lips feel swollen with the salt as I swim along here in the Floridian gulf, grateful for the added flotation from these saline surroundings. I have often thought it would be interesting to swim in the Dead Sea. I float easily as it is, and can imagine that maybe I could even walk on the Dead Sea.

I think of how dead I began to feel after years of marriage, along with four children. Though each child was an absolute blessing to me, I found myself exhausted and depressed at the age of 35. I felt very old. It was at this time that I rediscovered swimming. I'd been swimming, or rather playing in the water for 32 years, but only occasionally at best. I had not been serious about any exercise.

I learned at the ripe old age of eleven that exercise kills.

My dad was 44 years "young" when he died at his office in Valley Forge, Pennsylvania. The story went that he had just finished doing 40 pull-ups on the frame of his door, then keeled over with a massive heart attack.

I took up swimming seriously in that 35th year of my life, and I look at this period as another one of those great dividing lines, a new era, a better era. Finding swimming again gave a whole new dimension to my weary world. It revitalized me, and my kids can attest to the fact that it made me a better mother. Coming back to swimming was a connection that led me back to my dad without my even realizing it.

By the time I was 40, swimming a mile straight was like breathing for me—easy enough that I didn't even have to think about it. It was at this time, a fellow swimmer at the Bally's club I swam at, pointed out that I had a fast mile time. He taught me to do a flip turn and then encouraged me to compete in the Masters Swimming State Meet.

So I swam my very first swim meet (the first of many) in 1997. I swam the mile and the 1,000 yard events and won a gold medal in both events. The bug bit me big time!

Other than competing in a couple horse shows when I was in middle school, I never had the great opportunity to experience real competition (other than the years of competing I had with my siblings, vying for parental attention). There had been a diving contest during those weeks of diving lessons, but I was the only girl competing with a couple other guys, so it didn't feel like a true competition.

Coming back to swimming provided a much needed boost to a very low self-esteem, and I also believe it's what got me through a long, drawn-out and painful separation and divorce.

There are all sorts of things one can turn to when faced

with trauma. I'm thankful I turned to this outlet.

*****

After the last turn, heading toward the beach, I feel that added kick of adrenaline as I anticipate finishing this, and moving on to the next step.

In almost every triathlon I've done, the last leg of the swim is where things get easier. It takes me a good 800 meters before I feel warmed up. And this is where I start passing those swimmers that aren't used to either the longer distances or who started out too hard. I enjoy gliding past people and feeling the strength in my arms with each stroke.

The sun shines in sheets of glass, cutting through the clear green salty realm on this fine November day. In this moment I am at peace. I love the way the sun and water interact. The warmth and brilliant light are so welcome after spending the last month training in a Michigan lake.

Most people don't swim in lakes up north at this time of year. There have been many moments this Fall, swimming in a cold lake in Troy, where I've seen people dressed in their sweat shirts and jackets standing along the shoreline shaking their heads, staring at me and my friends with a look of disbelief.

Yes, we are crazy. But I don't think there is any other time I've ever felt so alive, so invigorated as I do when I swim in that 50-60 degree water. I am shockingly alive! I've learned to appreciate any patch of sunlight that falls on the surface and cuts through to give a moment of warmth. The sun sits low, and as the weeks progress into autumn the patches become fewer and fewer. Swimming in and out of them becomes a game, in and out of the light. When I die I probably won't hear voices saying "Come into the light." Instead they'll be softly saying "Swim into the light, Martha!"

There is little noise now here in the Gulf. The breathing, the splashes as my hands reach in and out, the muffled kicks in a rhythmic pattern, all contribute to a symphony of soft sound. There is such a music to the underwater world.

Sometimes I sing when I'm underwater. One day back in the summer, I spent the entire length of a mile long swim singing Italian opera ad-libbing most of it. Cold autumnal swims however don't inspire singing, only shudders and yelping, and I wonder at times how far the sound travels underwater. Could my friends hear the gasps? Were they making their own?

Recollections come of times spent underwater in our in-ground pool in Pennsylvania. My siblings and I would play games. We'd get in the corners at each end of the pool and yell things as loud as we could, and see if the others could decipher any of what we were saying. As I recall, we couldn't decipher much, but we could hear the yelling.

There were many games of Marco Polo, where one kid was "it" and had to swim around calling "Marco" with eyes closed, trying to find the others as they called out "Polo." We were lucky not to have had any serious accidents.

And then we'd play the tea party game. We'd let all the air out of our lungs, try to sit on the bottom, and mimic the motions and gestures, lifting the tea cups, pretending to have polite conversation. It was such a short period of time, the length of a good breath of air. And yet in reflection, that time is suspended, hanging preserved in the alcoves of my mind.

There are so many good pool memories, crystal clear and blue, when the sun was always high in the sky. Or the hot, sultry nights when sleeping was impossible, and we'd take sudden runs down the hill with towels flapping like wings, down to the pool in the dark. We had no lights, but that didn't deter us.

Every time I swim now, I feel I honor this person, my father, who introduced such a special world to me. I see the gentle strong arms and hands...I watch my hands stretch before me into the water. I'm so close now, to those wonderful memories, and to the finish of this swim.

*****

I complete my swim in one hour and six minutes. I run out of the water with a number of other dazed-looking comrades, wondering what their thoughts were through this wild adventure we've shared. We run through a chute and across a mat that beeps to confirm that we have successfully completed this portion of the race.

Though I am happy to have finished this portion of the race, there is a part of me that hates to leave the water. So often I hesitate to get out of that environment. When I am in that aqueous atmosphere I feel I have come home after a long, dry, stretch in a desert of distractions. Any worries of the day melt away like the early spring rivulets running down the mountainside.

We crave water. We love to listen to a babbling brook, the powerful ocean sound, a waterfall, a fountain, or the soft rainfall on a summer day. We've even created machines to mimic the sounds. We come from a place of water. The first nine months of our existence are spent in that warm, wet world, and 75 percent of our makeup is fluid. How do we as humans get so far away from what we are, from the substance that we come from?

When I get out, I feel as though I've become a lumbering sea lion, suddenly awkward and heavy. It's hard to believe that such great, clumsy creatures can become so graceful and lithe once submerged.

*****

Today though, I'm glad to be out. I'm glad to be the lumbering sea lion. Like the tadpole morphed into a toad I'm now glad to be on land. This was like no other swim I've done before. And soon I hope to have that gazelle-like feel to my legs again, to leave the water behind me like leaving my bed in the morning, bounding forward to the day ahead, and then I'll return to my beloved, watery world when the time is right.

I finish the swim—a landmark on its own. 2.4 miles of swimming is nothing to scoff at, and everything to feel good about. I've accomplished something that so few will get the chance to experience. And yet, this is only the beginning!

Now, just another 112 miles of biking and 26.2 miles of running (or walking!) lie ahead of me.

Chapter Two:
T-1

"Confidence will make you, Fear will break you."
—From a letter Dandridge wrote to his sister, Aubrey
April 25, 1944

T-1 in triathlon is the transition period between the swim and the bike portion of the race. The word transition means the process or instance of changing from one form, state, activity, or place, to another.

To run out of the water and get my legs working underneath me again is a challenge. Changing from sea-legs to land-legs is quite the shift in activity. The lumbering sea lion returns.

And though the transition part of the triathlon is a small portion of the race, it's a very significant one. There is a real art to it. In training, one can't forget to work on this all-important part of the race.

The pros have it down to a real system. There are all sorts of tricks one learns after a first triathlon—things like having the sunglasses in the helmet sitting on the handle bars, and having bike shoes already clipped onto the pedals with rubber bands holding them in place. Stretchy race laces for your running shoes leave no need to stop and tie them.

When I first began doing triathlons, I thought transition might be a time to take a breath and pause for a moment, but there's no such chance. You quickly switch gears from swimming to biking, biking to running. No time to even think, let alone a pause! Almost immediately, I realized I'd gotten myself into a sport no person with ADD should ever be involved in. So many things to remember!

I run through the chute lined with many spectators and pull off my cap and goggles. The feeling of pain in one eye with the release of suction reminds me that the long battle I just finished was probably nothing compared to what lies ahead. But being a silly, vain, woman, I still wonder how deep the lines are plastered into my face, and how long it will take for that 'not enough sleep' look to fade. (In later years, my granddaughter would call it the " beef jerky" look.) I can't tell you how many times someone has asked me if I hadn't gotten enough sleep the night before, when I'd only just gotten done with a swim, and was feeling full of energy.

I listen for my sisters, hoping to hear them yell my name so I can locate them.

My older and younger sisters, Jency and Cathy from Philadelphia, met me down here in Florida to support me during this all-day event. It's nice to know there will be someone to catch me when I collapse at the finish line (if I'm lucky enough to make it that far), and help me struggle back to the condo we rented for the week. Running with my heart wildly pounding in my chest, I wonder if this is really the way to spend a "vacation" at the beach. We could've just come down and laid around the pool or on the beach, reading books or taking casual strolls, collecting sea shells and beach glass like

SEARCHING FOR A MAN OF IRON

we did when we were younger. We could have jumped off bal-
conies into dunes of sand, or walked to the nearest sundries
shop to get licorice in flavors of strawberry, chocolate, and the
true black. We could have climbed on jetties to find starfish,
or gone crabbing and fishing in the bay, or built elaborate sand
castles at the edge of the water. Wouldn't it have been so much
more relaxing to just stand in the surf, jumping the waves, or
body surfing them into the shore? But no, I chose to fill my vacation with something so strenuous that my doctor recom-
mended I have a stress test and electrocardiogram just to make
sure I was in good enough condition to handle it.

I feel the presence of my siblings, but I don't see them. It's
nice to hear your name called out when you're racing. You become such a part of the whole conglomerate of athletes, all
working together, in a mass of energy, that to hear your name
reminds you that it is an individual struggle. Ultimately, you
have to accomplish it on your own.

There is a haze of activity—hands waving, clapping,
cheering, yells, and background music as I head through the
free standing showers. As the warm spray hits me, it summons
up the sensation from all those nice hot showers at the beach
houses we stayed at when I was growing up.

That warm and fuzzy feeling of standing there in the semi-
open air rinsing all the sand of the day away comes back. The
soothing spray on my head covered me with such a sense of
well being. In those moments all was right with the world.

From the time my family moved to Pennsylvania in 1960
when I was six, to when I left in 1974, just about every summer vacation was spent at the shore. And of all the places we
ever stayed at, the shore houses, cottages, camp grounds, ho-
tels, motels and cabins, the blue house in Harvey Cedars, New

Jersey, stands out as a pinnacle. Like an open trunk of golden treasures, spilling over with many of my richest childhood memories, it was symbolic of all the healthy things you find in a family. My mom and dad were both relaxed. It was a time to kick back and enjoy. The daily chores of getting kids off to school and running the household, and the headaches from work worrying about how to save the world, were put on the back burner.

What is it about the beach at the ocean? Is it that feeling of realizing you are just this tiny grain of sand, a minuscule speck in the grand scheme of things? Is it being near this earth-covering body of water, and in the effects of its enormity and power you realize that nothing is really under your control? Or is it the nights filled with stars, more stars than you could ever see in your light-polluted cities, inducing a mind-boggling wonder at anything or anyone that could come up with this idea of creation?

Yes, life was carefree at the beach, but of course with five other siblings, there were always the little spats over who gets the shower first. It was often a race from the beach.

*****

Not unlike today! I come out of the showers, appreciating that we got such a nice day for the race. I hear two people yelling at me to, "Lie down!" and in a flurry of activity I have these two grab me unzipping my wetsuit from behind and starting to peel it off, again yelling, "Lie down."

I dutifully obey and they finish the peeling process, pulling the wetsuit off over my legs like I'm some banana.

I smile and chuckle, thinking about what the race director

said to us in the meeting yesterday. "And make sure you wear a bathing suit underneath your wetsuit." He laughed as he continued. "Yes, we have had people not wearing anything underneath." It was actually written in bold capital letters in our race book "NO PUBLIC NUDITY PLEASE." We're so serious about this in our country here!

A big thing I've learned in this world of training and racing is to let go of some of the Victorian, prudish ideas and attitudes I grew up with. Having grown up in a church school, I'd learned to be very modest, mortifyingly so. So when I was reunited with swimming, and then added on biking and running after all those years of modesty, I quickly learned to relax and not worry about running around half naked, exposed for all to see, and even being photographed! I'll never forget the expression on my teenage children's faces when they realized their mother would be running around in nothing more than a bathing suit and running shoes.

Talk about a transition!

You learn the body is a fine machine, and it can be trained to do amazing things. Growing up in a Christian school environment, we were taught to not put emphasis on the physical. It was all about the spiritual. But the more I've developed in my training, and the more transformed I am physically, the more in touch with the spiritual I've become. The more I've learned about the finer details of this corporeal structure, the more in awe I am of what a masterpiece each one of us is.

The body really is a temple, to preserve, to cherish, to house our most precious gift, our spirit, our soul. To train, to build, and to define the muscles, to turn them into powerful tools, to have the body work like a well-oiled machine frees our spirit. A Feng Shui for the body; when everything is in its right place, energy flows through without blocks.

There is a high level of respect for what this flesh and bones can do when competing in races of this caliber. I have never felt naked in these settings, and I've never felt that sense of a guy leering at me, even though I'm only wearing a skimpy bathing suit.

I perceive a sense of equality that I don't get in any other arena in life. No matter what our gender, race, or age, we are all reduced to the same machine-like motions, but with a great spirit and will that makes us all one and the same.

One of the reasons I decided I could attempt this inconceivable feat of Ironman is that I went through a three-day labor with my second child, Eva. If I could go three days without eating or sleeping, Ironman should be a piece of cake! It's only one day!

I've often thought the comparison between endurance racing and childbirth is eerily similar (although my mom's half-hour labor with me would've been a sprint distance event!).

Yes, they are quite similar, only you have hundreds or thousands of other people enjoying the experience with you. All in labor together!

And I would say, the end stages of an Ironman, or even a marathon, are so like that transition period at the end of labor, it really makes me wonder why anyone would willingly put themselves through it. Surely, it's for that feeling you get when you cross the finish line, or that moment of birth, the feeling of euphoria, and the blissful amnesia that follows. It's for the wonderful loss of memory of the hours of pain and grueling work that you just experienced that envelopes you and leaves only a deep sense of satisfaction.

I like to point that out to the male athletes, "That's what

it's like to have a baby!"

*****

I'm jolted back to the present as a volunteer hands me my wetsuit. I head along the path lined with makeshift fence, a series of bars with all the advertisers' products and logos hanging down like banners. I hear the upbeat music and the announcer's voice over the loudspeaker adding to the excitement.

Up ahead in the transition area I see the giant green Gatorade bottle filled with air, and a little beyond that the equally large Timex air-filled watch. We received nice white ball caps with the Timex logo on them in our race packet bags. I placed mine in my bike-to-run bag for that long run ahead of me today. I run past the many rows of orange-colored racks with the numbered bags on them.

I see 1931, the number I marked on all my gear: my wetsuit, helmet, bike, and labels on all of my special needs bags, and the clothing in them.

It's the number of the plastic timing chip on the band I fastened around my ankle before leaving the condo this morning—double checking the velcro to make sure it was secure. This all-important chip records your time at each checkpoint during the race, and other than the silver ID band they fastened on my wrist at registration check-in three days ago, is perhaps the most important item to be wearing.

Today, I am athlete 1931, the number that was written in permanent marker on both my biceps muscles this morning at 5:00am.

It seems so long ago, and yet it has only been three hours.

I love that quiet time of body marking before the sun has risen. The dark silhouettes of palms, some with white Christmas tree lights, stood perfectly against the still morning sky. That hour holds such promise and potential for the rest of the day.

The smell of permanent marker is forever a reminder of any triathlon I've ever done. The numbers marked on my legs and arms are a keepsake I used to hang onto for days after my first races. It always felt like such a badge of strength, fortitude, and courage. I liked to hang onto that euphoria of glory for as long as possible.

Or perhaps the numbers are just a little indicator that I am one of the few crazies that do this sport. I've seen some Ironman athletes end up with white number marks left on their arms when the marker has prevented the tanning of their skin. They also mark the back of your calf with your age, so you always know if the person you are passing, (or who is passing you) is in your age group.

The age groups are divided into five year increments: 20-24, 25-29, etc., and then also separated into male and female. It provides a more level playing field when you are competing and getting awards in your age group. A 60-year-old can't fairly compete against a 20 or 30 year old, although I know quite a few older athletes that hold their own against the younger ones.

I've had plenty of older athletes pass me, and I've passed many that were younger than me. Last year at the Ann Arbor, Michigan Triathlon, running through the woods on the challenging trail portion of the race, I came up on a guy with a 40 on his calf. And when I passed him I heard him mutter, "I should trip you." But then he laughed, and I knew he was kidding. I continued with a smile in my step, feeling grateful that

I'm able to do this at my age. Who would've thought!?

1931....my dad would've been ten years old in 1931. I think back to my tenth year, to a vacation at Lake Wallenpaupak. My dad and I were out in our red canoe on the water. He gave us that canoe as a family Christmas gift, and I can still remember him painting the white letters of the name on the front.

I remember this perhaps a little more vividly than my siblings, because I had left my new bathrobe on top of the canoe while the letters were still wet. The letters stuck to it, and I received one of those individualized reprimands. Daddy named the canoe "Discovery" because he had bought it with $100.00 he earned by selling an article to Discovery Magazine. It was a fitting name for this conduit to exploring. And what was a perfect name for a canoe has become an equally fitting name for the shuttle carrying man out to space. Dad would've liked that.

We paddled all the way across the lake together, about a mile in width. Then suddenly, he put down his paddle and said, "You can paddle us back now." I remember feeling a little startled, taken aback. Surely I didn't hear him right. Did he really expect me to paddle us back on my own? He lay there with a big smile on his face, the sun streaming down on us in all its glory, shining in his black and white hair. I realized he wasn't kidding. So I started paddling.

Now, if someone were to tell me this story, yes, I might think it verging on abuse to expect your child to paddle you around the lake. But the satisfaction I got out of that moment in time, knowing my dad thought enough of my abilities to get us back across the lake, felt so good. It became one of those classic moments to fall back on whenever I doubted myself.

Someone believed in me, and other than God and myself, it was perhaps the person I most needed to believe in me.

I have loved canoeing from that day on, always feeling appreciation and confidence with each stroke I take.

*****

I head to the female changing tent, a big white "circus" tent, and I hear all the volunteers calling out, asking me if I need any help. In an hour and six minutes (an hour and 14 minutes under the cut-off time), I managed to be the 385th athlete out of the water, passing even some of the pros. I relish this moment of being near the top, as I know I will quickly lose this status being the poor cyclist that I am. And I feel very catered to with all the attention from the volunteers. As more and more athletes fill the tent there will be less individualized attention, so I appreciate this moment of glory, but try not to bask too long.

I thankfully decline the numerous offers and go about my business of changing. I'm grateful for little things like dry clothes to change into. The pros and some of the serious age-groupers don't waste the time changing. They take off in the bathing suits or one-piece tri suits as soon as they've rinsed off and grabbed their gear. But after swimming in salt water and knowing I've very little chance of coming out in the top by the end of the race, I opt to be comfortable and dry, even if just for the moment.

After peeling off my wet bathing suit, I put on my dry, red tank top with the handy, dandy pocket on the back with the GU (an energy gel with a consistency like toothpaste) tucked in it, and then my bike shorts. I pull on my socks and take off for the bike area. I feel like a new woman.

I run out of the tent and once more, two volunteers are yelling at me, asking me if I want suntan lotion. They stand there with their gloves on, poised and ready to slap on the thick, white cream with the summer vacation fragrance to it. What a luxury this organized event is—such royal treatment. It's almost like being at the spa! But once again I decline. I had planned in advance for this, actually visiting a tanning booth to change my winter-white skin to a more resilient tan, to protect me from sunburn. I tan easily when given the chance. I inherited my father's olive-colored skin.

But where did this olive skin come from? I wonder. My family tree takes me to all sorts of different countries: Germany, England, Scotland, Ireland, and Wales. And as far as I know, these are fair-skinned countries. Perhaps, as someone suggested, there was that stray Italian or Greek that snuck into the family tree.

My father liked to draw on his Irish and Scottish heritage, and thoroughly enjoyed Celtic music. He would honor those ancestral lines by listening to Irish music on St. Patrick's day, occasionally throwing in a little jig. He loved the Irish Tenors. I remember a time where he sang a rousing chorus of "Old King Cole" smiling, saying he was celebrating our English heritage. There is also a vague memory of some Scottish lullaby.Maybe it was "Sweet Afton", the song his father sang to him when he was a baby.

Sometimes in my longings for the presence of my dad, I'd picture him as some mythological being, because I never got to know him as just a regular human with all the flaws and imperfections. I saw him as a god. But perhaps in retrospect, not so much like the god Mercury or one of those well-known gods. In light of the circumstances, he was more fittingly like the vaguely known Abandinus, a god known only from inscriptions near Cambridge, England.

My father didn't choose to leave us, but nonetheless, we were left behind with a great hole in the fabric of our family. The tapestry was torn, and in some spots left hanging by thin threads with no hope of ever being sewn back to its original state. No mending could resurrect the family to what it had been.

So I look back, searching, digging up relics of my past, insights into who this person was. And if it's only to place them carefully on the shelf of who I am, then so be it. I won't leave them covered or buried any longer.

My older brother, Stephen, has done a great deal of research into our heritage, taking us back to King Edward of England. I come from King Edward, the Plantagenots, the Howards, Dukes of Norfolk, from Macfarlans, Cudmores, Lochnars, Coles, Pendletons, and Davies.

We are even connected through marriage to Eunice Cole (luckily not by blood), a woman accused of being a witch in New Hampshire in the 1600's. Yet another thing I was teased about in high school, though there were some who hesitated, worrying I might put a curse on them. The poet John Greenleaf Whittier included "Goody Cole" in a few of his poems, writing of the curses she supposedly put on ships. Eunice Cole was jailed on the "just ground of vehement suspicion," but she was not found guilty. There was even a pardon for her in 1938, long after her death, which was no doubt a comfort to those in her bloodlines.

As I have been working to live more and more in the present, I have also, ironically, become more and more interested in my heritage. It's not enough for me to go back and look at pictures or names. I want to know their idiosyncrasies, their character, what made them "tick". I love tracing down the line and finding out what these people loved and who they loved, and even if they loved.

Cellular memory—those memories stored in every one of our molecules. Those moments of deja vu, feelings we've been here, done that, are stimulated and released from the mnemonic organisms we can't really even understand.

I grew up in a very cerebral environment in my family, and in my church. I was raised a Swedenborgian. It's been called a "thinking man's religion," very doctrinally based.

Bryn Athyn, a quaint little borough (yes, they still call it a borough!), fifteen miles north of Philadelphia, was founded in 1897 as a religious and educational community. The Welsh name means "hill of cohesion," and there on a hill sits a magnificent structure, the Cathedral, that looks as if it came right out of medieval Europe.

My father had moved here in 1928 when he was seven, and lived in two smaller houses before moving into a big home right at the edge of the Cathedral grounds.

Good old "BA", this is where I spent my formative years. I grew up thinking it was normal to hang out in gothic buildings of stone.

My great-aunt Clara and uncle Harold Pitcairn lived in one of the two castles that sat on either side of the Cathedral. The Cathedral, built in the early 1900's, was a place of worship. The two castles, called Cairncrest and Glencairn, were built as homes for the Pitcairn families. These stone buildings stood so stately on those hills of Bryn Athyn. And even today these three elegant structures remain almost untouched by the years since their inception. The timeless beauty has remained with me so deep-seated. I have wonderful memories of Aunt Clara's and Uncle Harold's hillside leading down to the Cathedral grounds covered with fragrant, yellow trumpet daffodils and white narcissuses. We were allowed to pick handfuls of the crisp, sweet-smelling signs of spring and the purple pansies that grew alongside of them.

There was a pool in the castle "courtyard," down stone steps with wrought-iron railings to a smooth stone pool deck. The pungent boxwood, beautiful rhododendrons, and lush green ivy softened the stone walls that surrounded the area. The pool was always a treat on a hot summer day. There was a secret room in the castle too, secret enough that I can't recall how we got into it.

The home my Cole grandparents moved into in 1938 at the other edge of the Cathedral grounds, though not a castle, was a stately abode. My grandfather, inspired by the castle names, would dub the home "Vinecurst."

There were beautiful lavender and white wisteria vines covering the stone walls at the corner of the house. He kept after those vines, claiming he had to "fight back the wilderness." He feared if he was ever to be sick for three days and not able to keep up with them, they'd come in the windows and choke him.

The stone paths lined with boxwood on the east side of the house were a favorite place to visit when the morning sun would grace the area. Running in and out of them, releasing that strong scent and the rustling sound, was where I wished to be. There is no "quietly" walking through the boxwood. But regardless of the noise, they were still good places to hide when bored with adult conversation.

When I picture that Cole home, I can't help thinking about a tale my aunt told me of a night when she was young and the town was searching for a missing boy named Theron. He'd gone missing that day, and the adults continued searching deep into the night. She said there was such an eerie feel to that night, and she could hear the haunting sound of the peacocks that were kept at Glencairn wailing through the night as she lay in her bed.

They finally found the boy. Sadly, he had drowned in Pennypack Creek.

And even though I wasn't there, I can hear those soulful peacocks wailing, and can imagine how eerie that must have been for my aunt as a child. I wonder about my father, and how it had affected him.

The Cathedral is a most impressive building, researched and carefully designed down to every detail. Every functional or decorative part of the Cathedral, right down to the doorknobs, is based on a representative inner meaning. Nothing was overlooked.

But as a child, none of that really mattered to me, or my siblings. Our concerns were more with the present, that world within our grasp.

I remember leaning against the shoulder of a parent, oblivious to the sermon, catching only words and phrases out of context, staring up into the colored light filtering through the beautiful stained glass windows in the Cathedral. This was a weekly routine, whether we liked it or not. To look up into the magnificent east window, the Lord's face so clear, so present with all 12 disciples underneath, how could one doubt his presence in that sanctuary. As a child, I just took it for granted. There were no questions...not then.

When I was growing up there in the 60's and early 70's there were about 2,000 people living in this close-knit society. It was almost as if there was a glass dome that covered and protected our little town from the rest of the world. There were stories and all sorts of rumors that circulated in the area surrounding our "village". I'd hear from friends I'd made outside of our community, questions like, "Were we all from Sweden?", or "Did some of us really have six fingers and six toes?" and my favorite, "We were a Cult!". Here was a beautiful, wooded, isolated community surrounded by Philadelphia suburbs. Yes, I could understand why people might talk about us, questioning who we were. But we were just a society that based our lives on looking toward God.

In many ways it seemed a magical little town, with almost a Brigadoon feel to it. But in later years, I would cynically refer to it as Mecca. Another phrase I would use, after having moved away, was that "all roads lead to Bryn Athyn." Many of the residents never ventured out, while those of us living all over the world would always "take the pilgrimage" back there for visits, or the final return after giving the "outside" world a chance.

Yes, Bryn Athyn is a quirky little town. And yes, there is that pull, that magnetic draw that always calls to me, beckoning me, talking me into at least one trip every year.

My siblings and I grew up learning Hebrew, Greek, and Latin. I can still sing any of those Hebrew songs we sang as little children. I learned a lot growing up in that atmosphere, how to think and what I believe.

"It's good to question and doubt. It only makes us stronger." I would hear those phrases many times from teachers and ministers. And I do value my upbringing, but after 14 years of living there, I broke away from the cloistered society and was glad to leave when I got married. And though I " broke away", I ended up joining a Swedenborgian group in the Detroit area, continuing a doctrinally dominated life.

One particular day in my adult life seemed to really hit me blasting through my inherited doctrinal mind-set. It was in 1990 at the funeral of an eight-year-old niece. We were at the burial, and I remember walking, almost floating across the field in that haze of shock, holding my own seven-year-old Amanda and five-year-old Adam by the hand.

Trauma wraps such a protective fog around us, like that soft blanket we were tightly swaddled in as a baby. It was as if we moved in slow motion, and the power of the moment hit me with a revelation. I realized, after years and years of learning, and studying all that doctrine, that it really is very simple. Life is very simple. It's about who you love, what you love, and how you love. But maybe I needed all those years of erudition to come to this realization. Maybe I couldn't have come to it any other way.

I also learned the importance of grieving and allowing yourself this most important rite. I had spent years in denial, completely shutting off that part of me that was my father, thinking if I shut it off it wouldn't hurt as much. And the church society at that time seemed to focus on the afterlife—not how tragic it was for us to lose our father, but how wonderful that he was needed in Heaven. I don't really blame the church. It was also the era. The field of psychology has taken great steps forward since the 60's.

When my niece died, I felt the temptation to flip that switch and shut down. It would have been so easy, but instead I allowed the feelings to come, welcoming them.

I know now that grief is a blessing, and I celebrate it. The level of grieving only indicates the level of love. Allowing yourself to grieve actually frees you up to live in the present. Denying it only holds you back.

Hmm...another big transitional moment!

*****

I run toward the bike area, mentally preparing myself for what will be the greatest challenge of this race...the bike!

Chapter Three:
The Bike

Tasting Honey

*One drop, one taste, the memories flow
releasing an ineffable power. Golden sap from
unknown flowers, healing for the wounded blow.
Bitter taste of the aspirin swallowed leaving no
remains of sour, for the sunshine in that golden hour
and paternal love from so long ago. Forever held
upon my tongue, takes me back through Time's portal,
to a place forgotten, when I was young, to a face
that holds my very soul, to those hands from which
my heart has sung of nurturing captured in amber gold.*
—Martha Cole Childs, 2006

To bike, or not to bike. Like some modern-day Hamlet, I would ask this question during the months and months of training. Any of my friends will tell you I am not a big fan of biking. I bike because it's part of the triathlon, but if I had a choice, I might prefer swimming or running 112 miles. Okay, maybe not. It would take too long. So I'll accept the biking as part of this race.

We had to set up our bikes in the transition area yesterday. I taped six power bars in three different flavors to the bar between the seat and the handle bars. And in my Bento box (a thin black box strapped on where the handle bars and middle bar meet) I put a Chapstick and some salt tablets, with room for more later on. I placed a garbage bag over it all to keep it dry overnight.

With an Ironman race, you have to arrive days in advance to check in. And it's a good thing too. You are better able to acclimate when the weather conditions are so different. I left cool and even cold temperatures back in Michigan. Here in Florida, it's downright balmy, with temperatures expected to go into the 80's with high humidity. I don't relish the thought of running in 80 degree temperatures. I much prefer 50's or 60's for running. Too bad we couldn't run first. But for safety's sake they have to have the swim portion first as there would be a danger of losing too many tired athletes if it were the other way around. So yes, it makes perfect sense to have it in the order it is. It's very difficult to drown while you run, no matter how tired you become. Though there have been moments when taking a "swig" of water or Gatorade and choking on it in my haste that I felt I could've drowned!

This morning I filled the tires with air, removed the garbage bag, and put a peanut butter and jelly sandwich—cut up into bite sized pieces—into my Bento box. I looked at my shiny blue friend, patting the saddle. Yes, today it would be my friend. I'd spent so many hours of training on it we'd almost become enemies. There were days, after long rides where I'd envision throwing it over a cliff, even though there are no cliffs where I live, or in front of a truck. It's a bit of a love hate relationship. When I'm sidelined by running injuries, though, I'm madly in love with my bike.

There's a magic to the air before a race like this. I had walked into the transition area earlier with two other female athletes this morning who were probably in their 20's. All of us were first timers. We were discussing what the day before, and the morning of a race are usually like. "I'm always crabby and have a million and one reasons or excuses why I don't want to, or shouldn't do the race," I said. We took turns coming up with a whole list of complaints. "It's too early in the morning!" "I'm tired." "I feel like I'm getting sick." "My leg (or some other part my body) is sore." "I have too much to do." "My family thinks I'm nuts!" And then I piped in with, "I'm too old for this." We laughed (nervously) at our lame excuses.

But the morning of Ironman is different. You've trained for a good six months to a year to get ready for this. It's not like the short distance races that require far less training to get through. It's a second job for at least four months. I asked my teenagers and adult children if I could have their permission to do it, as I knew it would pull me away from them. I told them it would be as if I was away for three or four months, and they'd be on their own. They all gave me their permission. Fifteen-year-old Adam excitedly said, "Go for it, Mom!".

My new found friends and I continued walking through the sea of bikes and I said to them, "This is the first race I feel like there are a million and one reasons why I SHOULD be doing this." One of the girls added, "Ooh, I can feel a tingle going down my spine!" We all felt that tingle run down our spines.

*****

Now here it is, the day of the most intimidating biking I will ever come across.

Running in my sock feet, I enter the bike area. It fills a large parking lot that is peppered with palm trees and grass strips. The whole area is surrounded by the makeshift fence that lined the path, but this portion is also covered with orange webbing. Bold white lettering on it boasts the big sponsor Isuzu. At one end, the rust-colored Isuzu Trooper SUV sits awaiting its new owner, the winner of the race.

I look over a mass of colorful, beautiful, and some very expensive bikes. I know people who have dropped eight thousand on a bike, and yet they'll still try to save money on race laces or a water bottle. Thankfully, the bikes are well organized into numbered racks, so it's not too hard to find my bike. Another benefit to having a fast swim is there are far fewer athletes to contend with.

After finding my bike, I pop on my glasses and helmet, careful to fasten the chin strap right away. The officials will disqualify me if I leave the area with my chin strap undone. I slip on my shoes and grab my "wheeled companion" off the rack and start to run. I pass through all the other bikes, bidding them fair adieu.

Out on the road, I hop on. And so it begins. I've such a long road ahead of me.

A wonderful lesson I've learned from participating in endurance events is NOT to look at the whole picture while doing it. I have to take it apart, break it down, mile by mile. The thought of biking 112 miles is more than daunting. I try to get the idea out of my head, and instead, just focus on the moment. I've learned a lot of "life lessons" in these races. The focus should not be on the end destination, but the journey along the way. Just enjoy the adventure.

As I head out from Boardwalk Beach Resort onto Front Beach Road my legs start pumping in what will be an endless dance of monotony. The clip-on bike shoes are another wonderful addition to my gear. Not only do I get power from the down pedaling, I also get it in the upward movement. And since the shoes are attached there are no worries of slipping off the pedals. You could call it the "cruise control" of cycling.

It's about 8:15am and I've got till 5:30 p.m.—more than nine hours to finish the bike portion. Barring any mishaps, I should be able to do it.

On my left, the gulf side, stand all the many high-rise condos filled with a variety of tourists. I wonder how many are athletes, spectators, and volunteers this week. They must get a lot of business out of this event. On my right, I pass by a strip of grassy sand lawns and ranch style homes.

I hear the soft cooing of a mourning dove. Immediately I am called back to lazy weekend or summer mornings of my younger days. The haunting murmuring of the gentle song lulls me into memories sneaking up on the quiet grey birds, or running around with a butterfly net in pursuit of an elusive swallowtail. Summer was synonymous with nature. I adopted many wild creatures during my youthful years in Philly.

There were wild rabbits I'd save from cats, nursing them back to health till they could be free again, and chipmunks I'd hand-feed from the stores of acorns I had collected through the fall. There were birds fallen out of nests and abandoned baby animals that always tugged at my own wild spirit. I caught a blue jay once when it somehow got trapped in our house. Even after that bird pecked me on the face I was still determined to save all creatures.

My dad and mom were good enough to let me bring all these wild things into our home, though once I was spanked for feeding a stray cat when told not to. Nevertheless, that grey cat became a pet which I ingeniously named "Grey cat." Little did I know back then, according to T. S. Elliot's *Naming of Cats* that they prefer more dignified names. Grey Cat went on to give us many more pets with equally clever names like Lucky and Bunco.

Of course we also had the traditional family dogs, Ragazzo and Arffer. But I preferred the cats over the dogs because of their independence.

Odd names for pets was apparently an inherited trait.

My father's family had a dog named Twistle. He was a cute little white dog with a curly tail. They named him after the Deanna Durbin song "I Love to Whistle" combining the "to" and "whistle". My dad loved to whistle. It seems as though whistling is a lost art, much more popular a generation ago. You don't see as many people just peacefully whistling away. Is that because our society is more uptight? I wonder.

I think of the entertainers of "yesteryear" like Bing Crosby, Fred Astair and Danny Kaye, picturing them whistling away in movies and shows like the Danny Kaye variety show, a show that my dad loved watching. It aired at 10:00 p.m. on a weekday night. I would sneak downstairs in our Cherry Lane home and hide behind one of the livingroom chairs to catch a peek. But I could never fool my dad. He always knew I was there. He'd let me come out and watch the show, usually sitting in his lap.

I loved that show, and I adored Danny Kaye. I even wrote to him when I was nine letting him know that I played guitar and wrote songs, just in case he needed more talent on his show. I received a nine-by-eleven inch black and white picture with an autograph, but sadly I never did get that call to appear on his show!

*****

Here on my bike enjoying the sun and feeling my skin warming up and drying out, my thoughts quickly turn to one of my favorite subjects: food. I have been drawn to food for as far back as I can remember.

One of my most vivid memories of Colorado was a time I hid behind one of the thick, dark, wooden doors in our house, eating a smuggled piece of white bread with butter and sugar on it. And though that picture makes me gag now that I eat a much healthier diet, it is still such a cherished memory.

As it was, I never had to worry about weight control when I was growing up. I seemed to be one of those lucky few who could eat whatever they wanted whenever I wanted and never put on weight. I was a wisp of a child, the skinny kid everyone teased, saying things like, "If you turn sideways you'll disappear." In high school there was a game of who could put their hands all the way around my waist. Clothes never fit me. It was a struggle to find something that wouldn't slip right off me, or look like I was engulfed in fabric. And there was that infuriating nickname I hated so much: "Mac the bean pole." Some days, I wished I could just turn sideways and disappear.

*****

I reach down to grab my water bottle thinking it will be good to rinse away that salt water taste. I smile remembering a tale a fellow triathlete told me of how he cleverly packed his food in his water bottle and left the top off for easy access. Then, needing to relieve himself, he did so while biking along as so many serious triathletes do, forgetting he had put the food-filled water bottle in the water cage right bellow him. Being an older athlete he laughed it off and attributed it to senility.

I also recall an article I read in *Triathlete Magazine* about a pro triathlete who described a time he was biking along and felt a welcome spray of fluid on that hot day. When he realized it was the athlete ahead of him relieving himself it was not so welcome after all. Yes, there are those that take this business very seriously, not wanting to stop for anything. It can be the difference between winning and not winning.

I am not one of those. I will stop and use one of the port-o-potty's. This was a big issue in my mind before the race. Where would the port-o-potty's be located? Having grown up camping, I can't tell you the nightmarish outhouses we visited. And of course, there were also the times of using the great outdoors. I'm sure, being the tough army guy my dad was, he had no problems with this. Besides, he was a guy! Even though I was a "tomboy" I still had the delicate nature of a lady when it came to peeing outside.

I remember a particular trauma on one such trip. We were traveling along the highway and there were no rest stops. After I had whined and complained that I could hold it no longer, my dad stopped and told us to run into the woods. I ran in and found a private little spot in this wild area, surrounded by some bushes. I dropped my drawers and proceeded to squat, when I heard a loud grunt that scared me half to death. I turned to see an enormous black and white pig that, in my terror, looked more like a rhinoceros, so close I thought I would have a heart attack! I jumped up and ran until I got far enough away to safely look back and realized there was a thin wire fence keeping this creature at bay. Ever since, I'm never relaxed when I use the great outdoors. I still half expect a giant swine to leap out at me. A port-o-potty is a welcome sight!

This was such a big matter before I set out to do this race, but now it seems an inconsequential thing. There are more pressing things, most importantly, will my short legs hold out? Will I have anything left to give for the long run? And will my poor butt be able to stand sitting on this tiny seat for longer than I've ever done? When I think of sitting on this six by nine-inch triangle for what will be hours and hours, I wonder, who in their right mind does this?

*****

In training I am guilty of never biking more than a 90-mile stretch. Today will be new territory for me. I will go places I have never been, to those inner energies in the recesses of my spirit—places in the mental realm, not the physical. They say these kinds of races are 10% physical, 90% mental. And I know from some of my longer training sessions, that this is true.

Once again, I can't help but wonder about similarities between taking part in intense athletics such as this and serving in the armed forces. I've had many moments of questioning if this whole thing as a way to better understand what those in the armed services might experience. In both, you strip yourself of so many of life's comforts and conveniences, and are reduced to such basics of survival. Thankfully the aspect of having to kill is not a part of racing (though at times there is that urge to "crush" your opponent, or at least whoop his butt!). I can't even imagine having to kill.

Many times I have worried about ending up dead, though, when pushing too hard. I think it's an ingrained response. No matter how I rationalize and know that I won't keel over and die if I exercise, that worry is there. After all, that's what happened to my dad. I hear a voice so often when pushing myself, telling me, "You're going to die." But I've been hearing it for so many years that I have learned to ignore it. Hopefully, if I ever am in a situation of real danger, my gut will tell me, "this really is it"!

It was a big landmark to get to and live past age 44—the age my father died. That little voice had me convinced I'd die by then because I was more like my dad than my mom. But I inherited my mother's low blood pressure, as opposed to my father's high. So I take a little comfort in that.

I may have been a tomboy when younger, but I never even owned my own bike. My dad taught me to ride, though, on somebody else's. I remember his hand on the back as he ran along, though, supporting me till I could do it on my own. I don't remember much more. Obviously I was not enamored with the sport.

I bought my first bike three years ago, a month before my first triathlon. It's a bottom of the line road bike, a beautiful, royal blue Trek 420, and I bought it not knowing if I'd even like the sport. But all it took was that first race to fall in love with triathlon.

I had a nightmare the night before that first race. In it, I knocked down a bunch of cyclists when I fell over. Perhaps it was inspired by a story a cyclist friend told me. He had pulled up alongside of a big row of cyclists on a ride, and, not being able to unclip his feet, fell over and knocked down the entire line like a stack of dominoes. He quickly got up and took off. Every person that passed him after that cussed him out. Hopefully I will not suffer the same fate here!

*****

Obviously my thoughts are distracting me as I suddenly drop my water bottle and it goes sailing out into the road in front of a very serious looking athlete. He has some choice words for me as he flies past, the swoosh, swoosh of his disc wheels now disappearing rapidly ahead. I realize I am in a place I don't belong, out in the front of a lot of good cyclists. Hopefully he will be the only one I anger. And thankfully I still have another bottle of water to get me through until I can pick up more at an aid station.

There are aid stations approximately every 10 miles on the bike course where I can get water, Gatorade, energy bars, GU, fruit, pretzels, and cookies. It sounds like a day of picnicking if you ask me! I also have my special-needs bag, and an extra tire tube in case I used the one that was strapped under my bicycle seat, waiting for me at the 56 mile mark. It's good to pack some stuff of your own as you can't always count on them having the stuff you want. In most races they only have that awful lemon-lime flavored Gatorade available. That stuff just resembles too closely what it looks like when you're done with it to ever be appealing!

I fly along, my bike carrying me over the miles, and am deeply grateful I found this outlet to get me through a very difficult time.

After 23 years of a struggling marriage, separation, and then divorce, I could have turned to all sorts of bad escapes. The depression that could have consumed me was clearly avoided by following this healthy avenue. The boost I got from the training and racing was a natural way to get those endorphins coursing through me, and a great way to boost my self esteem. I wonder how many people end up on antidepressant or turn to alcohol to numb themselves through similar traumas.

Many times, when I'm heading out to train, my kids have asked me, "Why don't you do something fun?" "Go out on a date." "Go to some social event and meet someone." They have no idea how much fun I am having when I go to meet someone to swim, bike, or run. I can't say I've had this much fun with a group of people since I was a kid. So often I've had a feeling of just not being able to fit in. I'm not into meeting women for tea, or going out to coffee. I'm not a big fan of socializing at church or parties.

But I feel very comfortable being a part of this active lifestyle, and perhaps a large part of it is being connected to nature again. I am a kid again. And this sport keeps you young, too.

There is a woman on the master's swim team I joined who is 96 years old and is as lively and young as many that are decades younger. And I also heard of a man at a swim meet in California who was 105 at the time of the meet. All inspirational athletes!

I have a training buddy, a "hero," who is in his 70's, and on his birthday, (usually falling on Labor Day weekend) he'll go out and bike however many miles he's turning that year. When I first met him, only a few years earlier, I guessed he was in his 50's (and even wondered if he was single!). When I found out that, no, he was in his 70's, right then and there I put him on the top of a now long list of heroes—people who have a drive in their senior years that I would be honored to achieve, even just in part.

There is an 82-year old gentleman, Norton Davey, doing this race; attempting to be the oldest Ironman finisher ever. I hope he succeeds.

I've no doubt my father would have been one of these. I could see him trying to be the oldest Ironman. He had that youthful, never-grow-old spirit about him, not unlike the character Myles in the book he loved when he was growing up called **Men of Iron**. And as it turned out, he never did grow old.

The day he died, after having identified his body in the morgue, his brother Bill had matter-of-factly stated to those around him, "Well, he's never going to get old!"

*****

After taking a quick little jaunt on Riviera Ave, then heading back on Back Beach Rd., we bikers head out onto 79, a two lane highway with a bike path alongside. Now is when it will start to drag. And I'm only about 12 miles into it!

Biking in most triathlons is a very lonely activity, unlike the mass cycling you have in bike races where drafting (positioning oneself directly behind another biker) is allowed. There are no great, flowing pelotons in triathlon The triathlon is a very individualized sport, and drafting is illegal. You get a three minute "stand down" penalty if caught drafting on the bike. There is a drafting zone seven meters long and two meters wide surrounding each cyclist. A cyclist has 15 seconds to pass

63

another competitor, 15 seconds to be in and out of that seven meter long area.

In my case, I spend a good deal of time in that little box watching cyclist after cyclist pass me. Once again, there are real drawbacks to being fast in the water, but not so fast on the bike. What was that I was saying about gazelle-like legs? On the bike, I am probably more like an elephant, or a turtle!

I've met a lot of interesting people in the last couple days, participants in this wild adventure, and now I see them pass by me, one by one. How they recognize me, I don't know. I'm beginning to think there is a big sign on my back saying, This is Slow Martha, here! because a number of people have said "Hi, Martha!" as they fly by.

I'm just starting to notice the "flora and fauna" along the roadside now. There are a lot of pines along the highway. Pines, brush, grass, sand, and yellow flowering plants are my companions now. There has also been an occasional Red Tail or Cooper's hawk overhead or on a fence post; all too quickly disappearing behind me. As much as I love being down here in November, I really wouldn't want to live here. I'm a four seasons kind of woman.

I was born in 1954 in Havre De Grace, Maryland where we lived on a farm. My dad worked at Martin Company as a weapons system analyst.

In the spring of 1956, with my two older siblings and with newborn baby Tom being carried in an empty encyclopedia box (were there car seats back then?), our family flew to Denver. My dad, along with 200 other Martin employees, had been moved out west to form the Space Division of the company. There he helped design the Titan II, which launched the Gemini space capsules.

In 1960 Dad had a change in company and position. He became a consulting engineer in advance planning at the General Electric Missile and Space Division in Valley Forge, PA. We moved to the Philadelphia area, where for fifteen years I would do most of my growing up. Finally, when I married, I ended up in southeastern Michigan where I've lived now for 26 years. All my homes have been in places blessed by the changing of seasons, and my whole life has been influenced by them. I can even see a pattern to my life, going through these cycles.

Is there anything more glorious and spectacular than the display of colors and the cool, crisp air of fall? Each year I swear the colors are better than the last. I love the echoing calls from the V-formations of geese, and even higher up the sand hill cranes fill the sky, on their way to warmth. Every warm fall day you get feels like a "bonus day" knowing what lies ahead. It is a time of year filled with as many emotions as there are colors on the trees.

I slide through that fall phase, winding down, turning more pensive, and yes, even melancholy, as everything dies off, curling into brown. I become more engrossed in reading, 'riting, and running (my three "R's").

And then comes winter. Some of my favorite runs have been with the snow gently falling. I love watching the groups of snow buntings flying in their carefully orchestrated maneuvers here and there through the park. Even the crisp, clear days with a -30° wind chill have a charm to them and inspire some warmth in me, though many of my running friends call me crazy for saying so. The wind whistling through the white pines with its high-pitched whisper is always music to my ears no matter how cold it gets.

I tend to put on the pounds in winter, storing it up for hibernation, obviously! Napping becomes a regular activity too. Can there be anything as cozy as curling up in a sun spot at the end of my bed on a cold winter day, especially after a long run out in the wind and snow?

Spring comes with such anticipation after the long Michigan winter. I look forward to the birds revisiting the park I run at in March on their migratory routes. I feel such joy in seeing the golden eye, buffleheads, and mergansers on their return north. And the red-winged blackbirds setting up their homes in the reeds and cattails is a sure sign that we are done with winter.

The trees start to bud, and green swallows all the brown patches left behind. I can hardly wait to get my hands in the dirt. With each flower or plant bursting through, with each bud opening, my heart opens with a feeling of rebirth and expectation.

And once summer hits, ah, summer... Forget being indoors. From sunrise, to sunset I want to be outside. I've even set myself up with a garden maintenance business so I can be where I need to be, OUT OF DOORS!

In summer, if I'm not working, I'm training. It's easy to head out to the park for a bike and/or run. And from the beginning of June to the end of September, sometimes even pushing into October, it's such a treat to swim in the lake. Forget pool swimming. Who needs the lines?

There's such a strength in the changing of the seasons, and the more extreme a season is, the more potent the effect. And there's a certain security in having the seasonal changes. Things change, but you know the cycle will always start itself anew. You can count on it.

There's also a lot to be said for the security of having a father around. This was never something I even thought about until I no longer had that perception of stability—the comfort and safety of a great protector.

My great protector took out nests of black widow spiders when we lived in Denver. And he was always on the look out for the rattlesnakes. We had an area of stones that he called "rattlesnake garden".

On a camping trip to the Pine Barrens in New Jersey Daddy grabbed a poisonous snake that had slithered into our canoe and threw it into the water with such finesse. It didn't even phase him. He didn't break a sweat. My dad was an army man. He was tough and confident. I wonder if he had any fears at all, or whether, through scarring and emotional trauma from his war days, he just learned to camouflage such emotions.

There was only one time I ever saw him break down and cry. It was one of those days that no one forgets. November 22, 1963, the day Kennedy was assassinated. I can still see my dad's eyes filled with tears. Such a cloud hung over that day. It was my younger brother Tom's 8th birthday, and somehow that was lost in the upset.

In Bryn Athyn, Pennsylvania, we lived in a home next to a big woods, complete with a stream. With my father's obvious love of the great outdoors, he always chose a home with a wooded area, or a large expanse of land. Once again, it was a necessity, not a luxury. We grew up playing in the woods, a world of fairylands and dirty hands. I treasure that glorious feeling of losing all track of time, being engrossed in some project like creating moss-covered landscapes, or damming up the stream, catching frogs, crayfish, minnows, salamanders, or even snakes.

I still fill with a childlike excitement and fascination when I happen upon any of these creatures today, although the idea of walking through bogs and getting covered with leeches clearly does not appeal to me anymore. I was not your typical little girl with her doll collections, though I did like dressing up to play in the dirt. I would much prefer watching a tadpole turn into a frog than playing with dolls, but I'm sure at the same time I was thinking about the frog turning into a prince. There were times I tested out that kissing theory on some poor unsuspecting creature. It never did work.

I remember days filled with projects like creating camp grounds in the woods bordering the property, clearing out individual camping plots, and pretending to run the place like some of the older, rough cut individuals we had met on our real family camping trips. And then there were days of just exploring, or listening to the stream behind both our homes in Bryn Athyn and Huntingdon Valley trickling over the rocks in a musically soothing pattern.

I was always looking for animals, and birds in particular. I was intrigued by wildlife from an early age. I still remember the very spot I saw my first green heron, poised and looking over the stream, ready to strike at the first wiggle of life. That determined, almost unreal look in its yellow eyes and the tilt of its dark-capped head stays with me still. It was all irresistibly enchanting.

This love was passed on to me from my father. And just like digging into the earth; discovering hidden secrets, the more I unearth about my dad, the more deeper connections I see. This love had flowed to him through his mother in that generational river of heredity. She knew the importance of life out in the open arms of Nature. She had a great affection for

God's true handiwork, particularly astronomy. I've been told it was not for the technical aspect of it, but for the magic of it.

My grandma "Werty" was the ninth girl in a family of ten children, the last being a boy. And unlike her other sisters, who all got degrees in English and history, she wanted to study astronomy and science. My aunt relates the story of how one night the nine sisters dressed in their very best for dinner, and all descended on their father to overwhelm and convince him to let the last sister study astronomy.

Wertha received a Bachelor of Science degree from Columbia University in 1914, and did graduate work under Prof. Samuel Alfred Mitchell at the University of Virginia from 1917-1918. My aunt also told of how my great-grandfather gave my grandmother a gun to carry on her treks up to the McCormick Observatory at night. On hearing this story, and others about how her mother loved climbing trees (even being up in one when a fellow came to court her), I know I come by this love of the outdoors so naturally, so readily. Even though I never really knew my grandmother and great-grandmother with them passing before I was three, I know them all the same.

I think of all the times I sat high in the tree tops as a child (and even as an adult), swaying with the wind, seeing for miles around me; I had no idea that this enjoyable pastime was a love inherited not just from my father, but also his mother and grandmother.

When my father was a little boy, he obviously adored his mother and connected to that love of nature. He told her he'd make her a coat out of moles he'd catch and skin himself. I can almost feel the soft moleskin rubbing against my cheek, made all the more plush and comforting knowing it was made by the little hands of someone you love. However, the animal activist in me is happy to say even though he did catch and skin some, he never succeeded in accomplishing the task.

The letters Dad would write to his mother from Camp Rucker when he was 22 would be filled with references to the nature around him. One such letter, written when he was "pretty well out in the sticks..." went on, "The flora is carboniferous and the fauna is predominately saurian." And then there were always questions about the happenings in the sky. He had times where he'd be the only one to be able to find his way through the woods at night, solely directed by the stars.

He wrote that the "city boys" were funny to watch and wrote of an incident about one of them out in the woods. The fellow leaned his rifle against a bush then noticed a snake coiled around the branches. I can hear my dad chuckling as he wrote, "He didn't stop running until he was about 30 ft. away and couldn't be persuaded to go back for his rifle." And further, "It was only a harmless black snake, but they thought I was slightly crazy when I calmly picked him up with one hand and returned the rifle with the other. They were sure the poor thing was poisonous (they thought his tongue was a stinger) and objected to being introduced."

Camping was an activity we enjoyed as a family. From reading the many boot camp letters, I can see how Daddy developed such a love for it. He wrote in great detail of his rugged experiences at Camp Rucker with the 297th Engineers, then with the 597th A/B Engineers Co. at Camp Mackall, North Carolina, and finally with the 139th A/B Engineers at Camp Forrest, Tennessee. He wrote of the physically and emotionally tough training, the long nights, the 15 to 18 mile training run/walks, the ditch digging, and the jumping out of planes. But unlike some of the other guys, he never seemed to mind it, and even at times, seemed to enjoy it.

On top of the many letters he wrote, Daddy took the time to write poetry and songs that would end up in a book called **Songs and Poems of the Paratroopers**. He spent most of his spare moments—what little time he may have had between bivouacs, training, eating, and sleeping—writing poems and songs. He sent them to his sister to type up, and in time they were put together, published, and sold.

There was even mention of his selling some to Wanamaker's, the big department store back in the 40's. I am filled with a sense of wonder and pride knowing and being related to this person who could exist in the gruff, grueling environment he was in and yet still see and portray the beauty of it. In one letter, he spoke of the elegance of seeing 500 or so paratroopers all jumping at the same time, the sky filled with the "Lotus blossoms drifting." He wrote, "It looked like a fairyland." I am struck with the starry-eyed wonder, and perhaps naivete in this young man.

After living in the home on Cherry Lane in Bryn Athyn for four years, we moved to a two-acre property with the pool on Edencroft Road in Huntingdon Valley. It was a beautiful stone-sided house surrounded by gardens, with a hill in the backyard leading down to the pool and a wooded area. We moved in at the beginning of 1965, and that fall we lost my father.

It was three days before Halloween. It was not a happy Halloween that year, to say the least. And what followed seemed like many years of being in a haze. How does an eleven-year-old deal with something this big? They don't! I shut down and tried to stumble through the awkward years of becoming a teenager, and then the confusing adult years, getting married, moving to Michigan, and having four kids, all the while not really recognizing the tremendous impact that death had on my life.

It wasn't until recent years I realized the full magnitude of how a trauma like that had shaped my life. There was life before my dad died, B.D., and then after his death, A.D.. The dividing line is no less than the Great Divide, a milestone imbedded in my existence as if it had taken centuries to form. Yet it was as sudden as a meteor hitting, or a tsunami washing away every semblance of order and security. I think of earthquakes ripping apart the foundations of sturdy buildings, leaving only a pile of rubble, barely recognizable of its former structure. This was the force I felt, and nothing less.

Sometimes I wonder if it would have been easier if he had died after some long illness, where after months of suffering you may even welcome that final moment of life. But no, he went off to work, we went off to school, just another day... until it wasn't.

*****

I think the thing I don't like about biking is that life passes by quickly enough. I don't need to give it the extra boost of biking past it, too. "Life is evanescent. Here momentarily, then shifting, permuting, and always leaving something behind."(Samuel Johnson) Every moment should be cherished. How can one cherish things flying past so quickly you barely blink and they're gone? How so like hummingbird wings, flying so fast you barely see them. And only with patience do you catch the moment they light upon a branch or a feeder. You see the iridescent green of their feathers. Unless you take that time to stop and watch (or at least run very slowly past it), it slips away so quickly.

That's how I've felt about raising my kids. One day I was eleven, the next I have teens and even adult children! Where has the time gone? Time flies...like hummingbird wings. Even though it wasn't always easy raising kids, I cherish the experience, and still consider it to be one of the greatest highlights of my life. I've loved being a mother to my children.

I've read that you develop your parenting skills between birth and age five. My father and mother taught us well. She was a good mother to her little children. I can still feel the way she tenderly ran her fingers through the hair at the base of our skull. It was that special spot she always went for. I can hear the affectionate hum as she curled and twisted each strand.

Charlotte Ellen Davis, a statuesque beauty with dark hair and long legs, came from a family of seven. Her father was Edward Hugh Davis, and her mother Margaretha Lechner. She had older siblings Anne, Justin (who lost his life in the service in 1943), Dinah, and then a younger sister, Cathlin (Katie). This family also grew up in Bryn Athyn in a big, beautiful home on a hill leading down to the train tracks along the Pennypack River. I can still picture running down that hill into a blanket of fog at the bottom, yelling to my brothers and sisters, "Look I'm running into a cloud!"

My Grandma and "Papa" were still living there in 1960 when we moved from Denver. We lived with them for six weeks before moving into a studio apartment as a temporary home before moving into the house on Cherry Lane. And once again, thoughts of food take me back to my grandparents house. My grandmother had this wonderful ceramic chicken bowl, and when you lifted off the top of this coveted tureen there was always a plentiful supply of M&M's or other candies.

It amazed me that it never got broken with all the little hands always attacking it.

My grandmother obviously understood what was important to a child! She had that warm, loving sphere about her that welcomed you into her circle. For as far back as I can remember she had a Sunday night meal gathering, with any and all of the extended family invited. These Sunday night dinners continued right up until the time she became sick in April of 1981. She died that summer ending a tradition that held so many of us together.

Sometimes we don't realize what a powerful thing tradition is for pulling us together. We don't realize it until it's gone. Here after almost 20 years, I still pause on a Sunday evening and think how nice it would be to get together with all the family and have a bowl of split pea soup or spaghetti and Grandma's special homemade brown bread.

I see my mom with her bare feet tucked up under her, sitting in one of the comfortable livingroom chairs just relaxing, not worrying about having to take care of her six kids. We were all caught up in playing with our cousins, racing about the yard, or sitting around the TV in Grandma's bedroom watching "The Wonderful World of Disney."

My mom was the quiet, shy type, an extremely talented artist and musician who gave up the chance to pursue those avenues when she became a successful mother of six instead. She was always only one step away from being a kid with us. The memories of darting in and out of bushes and trees in Colorado on soft, pine-scented evenings, pretending we were rabbits hiding from the cars on the road, still stirs in me whenever I brush against a pine. And there was my mom, mother rabbit, hiding along with us.

She was the eternal flower child. Strains of a piano playing, and the sound of her singing songs like Mississippi Mud and Sunny Side of the Street, ring clearly in my head. She also played guitar and sang all sorts of folk songs, ballads, and lullabies. One of our favorites, "The Little Blue Man," was a bit of a strange song about an odd character, but we loved it all the same. And it became one of the songs I passed down to my children, despite its bizarre nature.

Mom had this wonderful little wooden music box, given to her as a child, that played eight different classical pieces. I'm certain that listening to this tiny treasure was where I first developed my love for classical music. Over the years, I've thanked her for this love of the classics, and she always replies, "You didn't get that from me!" But I know I did, even if it was just because of that magical little brown box.

I always felt that there were more lows than highs for me in raising my own children, but the highs were so much more powerful they easily outweighed the lows. I think of each of my children, two now adults, and know how lucky I am to have them. As of this month, I will become a grandmother. A GRANDMOTHER! I can hardly believe it. Surely I am not that old! When I think of the picture I had growing up of grandparents, none of those pictures included them on bikes or running. There have been times after a race when hobbling around where I might welcome the use of a cane or walker, and that's when I think, "yes, this is the picture I had."

*****

I'm getting white line fever here, pedaling along the endless two-lane highway. The sun is shining brightly, and it's starting to really warm up now. I'm glad to be moving along quickly enough to not worry about bugs, though I do get the occasional creature in my mouth if it's not kept shut. I guess I should stop talking to myself!

There is a gentle wind blowing, and I'm hoping we'll luck out and not head into a strong wind in the last stretch. A group of my friends and I biked the last 12 miles of the course the other day, so we'd have the feel for the portion coming in. It'll be great when I hit that spot, and know I only have 12 miles to go. Ah, but that's looking ahead. We mustn't do that. I'll look behind for a bit.

I'm reminded of trips along the highway as a kid. Trips that were only a couple hours in length seemed to drag on forever in our big station wagon filled with eight. There was always a fight going on, and I cringe to think of how not one of us was seat-belted in. How did we ever survive back in those days? I reflect on how different it was to have my four little children all strapped in, and yet we still had our share of arguments, flying fists, and crying. Some things never change.

How did my parents handle six kids? And even more importantly, how did my mom survive raising six of us after my dad died? I'm baffled when I contemplate what an incredible hand she was dealt. And four months after losing her husband, she also lost her dad.

My heart fills with such great sadness when I remember watching that sparkle in her eye fade, and seeing her carefree spirit put on hold. Mom wrapped herself in a protective screen. She is nothing less than a saint in my mind. Even with the wrenching heartache I felt as a kid, thinking about her losing her husband, I had no clue of what she had to face. It was only after having four kids myself, ending up divorced, and having to take care of their much-wounded needs, that I could have some insight into the depth of what she had to deal with... nothing less than a saint.

Those times through my teen years were so filled with turmoil. I think my siblings and I all turned to fighting and anger instead of dealing with our grief. And I know it's why I turned to alcohol and drugs in high school, to numb the perpetual ache. It was a very tumultuous eight years. I did not enjoy that part of my life at all. I know that adolescence and the teen years are a hard time for anyone, but to have the extra burden of unresolved grief weighing heavily on one's shoulders makes it even more difficult. And here my mom had to deal with six of us going through these stormy years.

*****

Occasionally, I see an athlete stuck on the roadside with a flat tire. When this happens, the athlete has to fix it, or wait for the tech support vehicles that come by every now and then.

As I bike past one such unfortunate fellow, I instinctively cross my fingers which are now nestled around the handles of my aerobars.

Aerobars give the cyclist the opportunity to become very aero dynamic. You lean forward with elbows comfortably resting on pads at handle bar level. One could almost take a nap in this position. And in fact, a cyclist friend told me about a man who, after biking some long miles, did fall asleep in that position. Luckily he sailed off into a grassy area where he fell and woke with a start! Oh, the pitfalls of long distance training! I have experienced a similar moment. Feeling tired after a long ride, I came into the parking lot of the park where I train—my home away from home—and as I approached my car, I carelessly looked down at my bike computer at the wrong time to check my mileage. I ran right into my car, hitting the back door with a denting thump, and toppled over onto the pavement. Feeling incredibly embarrassed, I jumped up and looked around to see if anyone else had witnessed such a ridiculous spectacle. Luckily it was one of those many days when very few were out there. I was okay, only a little wounded in my pride. My poor car, however, had a major crater in it. I dreaded the idea of taking it into the dealership where, only a week before, I'd gotten that same door fixed after my daughter's friend had backed into it!

When I did finally take it in, I could hear the ripple of laughter through the place as the story was relayed to all those guys who had fixed it just a week earlier.

Here on the highway, I hit some gravel, and again I'm worrying about flat tires. Please, please, don't have a flat. Even though it was something I did practice, I don't want to have to take the time to change a tire. I have brand-new racing tires, thanks to the guys at Bike USA where I got my bike. One of the owners generously gave them to me saying they'd gotten them in as samples. Since none of the guys at the shop were doing any big races, he was happy to let me have them. The Bike USA staff members were a great support to me and my biking. Always there to "take care of things a girl shouldn't have to take care of!" I guess I'm not quite as much the tomboy that I should be when it comes to cycling.

That's another thing about biking I could do without—all the technical stuff. If I wanted to be a mechanic, I would've taken up race car driving.

I try to cross my toes now too, but my Diadora bike shoes

are too tight. Curiously, my feet have grown since I've taken up all this stuff. I used to be able to wear size seven shoes comfortably, but now I need much larger running shoes to fit my feet once they swell after five miles or so of running. The bigger the feet, however, the better for swimming!

My feet are the only thing on me that is not petite in size. I sometimes feel like a duck when I run along. How I ever picture myself as a gazelle when running eludes me now, but I know I have had occasions where running along feels so easy that I do imagine thin, agile gazelle legs underneath.

Once, on a vacation in the Poconos when I was nine or ten, I remember running through the woods in a short, green dress, envisioning myself gliding along like some graceful antelope. In the very moment of that beautiful mental picture, I tripped and fell flat on my face. So now when the visions come I try to ignore them, fearing I'll end up tripping over my oh, so elegant ego.

As active as my dad was, I can't picture him on a bike or running. He did love the trampoline, and in Colorado we not only owned our own trampoline, but used to visit a place called Trampoline City.

I have vivid pictures in my head (perhaps because of home movies) of our trampoline in Denver. I see the pines and a cream-colored stucco garage with the curved orange tiles on the roof in the background. And I see my dad jumping in his special white pair of trampoline shoes, jumping, endlessly with flips, pikes, and twists thrown in. His white and black hair never became mussed, though on the downward jumps it flew up ever so slightly.

Daddy had a striking head of hair, not your typical salt and pepper. He had dark hair when he was younger until he went overseas to fight in the Battle of the Bulge. When he came home after two or three months of fighting and ended up in a convalescent hospital in Virginia, his black hair had white patches all through it. My heart aches when I think of an innocent young man who goes off to war, and sees things so unspeakable that it shocks the very skin of his scalp. A trauma so great as to change the color of your hair is inconceivable. The term "post traumatic stress" is just a label for something so unimaginable. Though his hair was black and white, I wonder if things could've been that simple, or whether all that he had to face in war came wrapped in thick, mind-numbing shades of gray.

We often wondered what happened to him to make his hair turn, but as children we never pried. There is a story of how he'd been asked to take a German prisoner to a camp, but be back in five minutes. The camp was 40 miles away, and that order left my father with a decision that no one should have to make. As the story goes, risking a court-martial, Dad ended up carrying the prisoner on his back the 40 miles to the camp instead of shooting him, and while he was gone his command post and everyone in it was destroyed.

For years I felt pride in thinking of him as a hero. But as an adult, not having him there to verify this story, my curiosity drove me to reading many books on the Battle of the Bulge, and even talking to other WWII veterans in hopes of having some idea of what had really happened. After speaking with a man who knew my dad for only one weekend during boot camp, I learned that, though they weren't together over in Europe, they were "never more than a few feet apart," and whatever he had suffered, they all had. Upon hearing this, I was finally able to let go of my quest, and realized that whatever happened, in the end didn't matter.

What those men suffered, they suffered together and many of them had to make decisions that only God should make. They are all heroes. I am left with a deeper respect and reverence now for any serviceman that puts himself in the line of danger to protect his country.

I think the only reason God allows people to experience the atrocities of war is to give them a glimpse into the basest, most evil side of human nature. We are all capable of violence, but we can choose whether or not to go to that smoldering side of our humanity. Some choose not to and end up dying at the end of a bayonet, knife, or gun. Even when killing is done out of self-preservation or protection, maybe a person can then realize something about themselves and our inherent nature, and in the end be a little less judgmental about others.

Daddy spent a few months in an army hospital in Virginia, where he would talk to the psychiatrist, very confused and conflicted. How do you obey people that tell you to kill? He would say "There is no such thing as a white lie." And he felt guilty for having survived.

But he still managed to muster up a sense of humor, no doubt more tinged with cynicism than before his days of battle. Having left behind the horrors in Europe, being asked by one of the doctors there why he wanted to go home, (as if a doctor really needs to ask that question!) he replied, "There's a roomful of pancakes I have to count."

When my father came home after his stay in the hospital, he walked in the kitchen door, burst into tears, and with a big jug of Mogan David wine shut himself away in his room for a month. He spent that long month writing a paper on cooperation.

He didn't smile for a year. Cooperation... if only life could be that simple!

*****

The shadow of a hawk crosses over me. I look up just in time to see it sail away across the blue—a red-tail. I love hawks, the way they seem to play with the wind currents, soaring up high, seemingly without a care. They keep a watchful eye, with their keen-sightedness and observation over all us land-dwelling creatures. I always look for them along highways, or anywhere for that matter.

I feel very connected with the hawk and sometimes a real kinship. Upon occasion, I've caught sight of one of those lofty creatures being attacked by a few (or many) smaller birds, and I have that "I know how you feel!" rise up within me. I watch as the hawk calmly ignores the distraction and persecution, just soaring on as if they aren't even there. I try to remember this when I'm in the same situation!

I wonder if my dad had any sort of connection to a particular creature. Surely he must have been drawn to one. He loved sea creatures like dolphins and whales. He talked about wanting to swim with dolphins. He told me a story one time about a dolphin saving a man's life.

He was very excited one day when on a walk down the beach on one of our seashore trips, he stumbled upon a whale vertebra. We brought it home and used it for a little stool for many years. (My older brother Stephen still has it!) The solid white chunk of bone stands about eleven inches high and eight inches in diameter. It was the perfect size for a child's stool, and I liked thinking of the giant it belonged to when I sat upon it. Of course there were always fights for who got to use it.

Desire for the whale bone or my dad's lap led to many arguments during the story times we were treated to on a regular

SEARCHING FOR A MAN OF IRON

schedule. Yes, regimenting even applied to story time. But oh, what a world that was! Story time was an opportunity to escape to many different places. The worlds that my dad took us to, carrying us off with that gentle nasal quality to his voice, were always an adventure. Sure there were the scary places we'd visit, but if there is a place more secure than that warm little perch on a parent's lap I would love to find it. In that protected space, with arms wrapped around you and the echoing voice as you lay your head against his chest—could there be a better spot?

We spent many hours in the land of Oz. My dad had the whole collection of Oz books, which took us to many more places than just the ones Dorothy visited in the movie! He even wrote his own version of the world of Oz, but wrote in each one of us kids as characters instead. Entitled, "The Ruby Palace," there was King Bingo, Queen Shar, Stephen as a prince, Jency as a princess, myself as a princess, brother Tom as a cowboy named, " Long Tom Shannon", my younger sister Cathy was a baby bewitched into a dinosaur! And sister Mary Jane was the two-year old blonde and blue-eyed apprentice to Glinda the Sorceress.

Thoughts of the book have come up often through the years. You don't forget about a book your dad wrote including you as characters, even if it never did get published. The two islands of Best and Worst in the Nonestic Ocean, with the age-old clash between good and evil, are places out of my father's head and heart—places my mind (and heart) visit from time to time.

I rarely thought of myself as a beautiful princess going through my life, except in the eyes of my father. I remember a time when I was in tears, sobbing away saying I was so ugly, and my dad comforted me, telling me the mirror didn't show the true look of my face, that it showed it backwards. And it didn't reflect my true beauty at all.

*****

I've been so lost in thought. I haven't been paying much attention to my surroundings along this highway. My one eye is still bothering me, and I know I've passed at least a couple aid stations. I think of the hawk's acute vision, and realize I've been struggling to see out of that eye. Being so wrapped up in moving and not stopping, it never occurred to me to have it looked at. Maybe I'll do so at the next aid station.

I carefully pull two GU out of my back pocket, open it up and try to chew on it, even though it's the consistency of toothpaste. I get bored with power bars and GU's. It's almost like the foods you get when you're sick-Jello, popsicles, chicken soup, ginger ale, all associated with that not-so-pleasant feeling. I'll never drink pop again. I haven't had any in 24 years now. I drank it for my nausea with my first pregnancy and that ruined it for me.

But this GU is made with honey, and every drop of honey that hits my tongue releases a vivid memory.

It was in Colorado. I'd gotten hit in the head with a baseball, and my dad crushed an aspirin in honey to mask the bitter taste. For some reason, ever since that moment, honey has reminded me not of the pain in the head that I felt, but the limitless nurturing I got in just a little spoonful of the golden amber. The five senses are great little prods to poke the deep interiors of our core, touching with an electrical charge, stimulating and waking latent thoughts and emotions. We can cover memories with years and years of forgetting, but still the prods can dig through. No matter how thick the layers become, a sensation can suddenly awaken, sometimes surprisingly, all sorts of vignettes from the past.

Chapter Four:
The Bike, Continued

"Walk down that lonesome road, all by yourself . . . "
—James Taylor

It's time to stop. I don't know how many miles into this I am, but I need to take a break and get off this bike, off the seat that feels molded to my butt, even if just for a moment. I see an aid station ahead with the blue and green port-o-potties, and all the dedicated volunteers lining the road.

I see the medics standing by their vehicle. I bike over, jump off, and ask them to look at my eye. The one guy takes a quick look, says it looks really swollen and asks if I need to quit. "Quit!? Quit!?" I repeat "Heavens no! There are just no mirrors out here. I wanted to know what it looks like! I needed to make sure that my eyeball was still intact!" I thank them, then run over to the port-o-potty, relieve myself of what little fluid I have, and I'm on my way again.

And back to the tedium...

Once again I hear a loud hello, and this time it's a friend from back home, a training buddy named Chris. Now here's another fine example of an older athlete, although "older" is becoming a more and more relative term! He's in the 60-64 age group. And this guy can cycle! I knew he'd be coming up on me. It wasn't a matter of "if" he could catch me, just when! And as swimming is my forte, cycling is his.

He'll be finishing his bike about an hour before me, no doubt. But I'll see him again out on the run. It's nice having a double loop course for the run. I'll be able to see where all my friends are in the race.

Besides Chris, I came down here with two other friends I train with in Michigan, Rod and Deb.

Of all the people I've come across in training, one of the most important connections I've made is with Deb. She lives on a lake about a half mile from my house. Discovering this person, and the lake right under my nose, was no less than finding buried treasure. The world of triathlon really opened up for me, not to mention finding a valuable friendship as well.

Deb has been doing this for a good long time, and she's just a young thing! She and I are within a few years of each other. When I think of how long she has been doing this before I even knew about it, I have to hold back from throwing myself to the ground on my knees, hands down, head bent over in admiration.

Her first triathlon was in 1978, right around the time this type of racing came into being. She is one of the originals, back to a time when there were no wetsuits and helmets were optional. Cycling is also Deb's forte. She laughs in her recollections of the leather helmets they wore. Now races are held just about every weekend in this area, but back then there were only two in the Michigan region, Waterloo and Traverse City.

I met Deb in 1999 through a friend, Ray, who I'd gotten to

know in the pool at Bally's. He said there was this great lake to train in right here in Troy. I remember Ray quoting to me, "People come into your life for a reason, a season, or a lifetime..." So true. So true.

Deb has said she was doing triathlon long before anyone knew what they were doing. And I have to say truly, "ignorance IS bliss." If I had known what doing an ironman race really involved, might I have reconsidered? Once again, it's like childbirth. If you really knew what you were getting into, being of sound mind, you would never do it! I'm thankful I didn't know.

*****

Now I'm here, very present, and areas that wish to remain anonymous are sore and tired. But I'm happy, and on a deeper level, loving every moment of the journey. The energy in a race like this is like nothing I've ever felt before. It pulls me along, props me up, and sometimes, gives me a little kick in the you know where! Support systems are wonderful things.

As much as I scoffed at the society I grew up in, there is a lot to be said for a community where everyone is trying to live a life looking to a higher purpose. And though it wasn't apparent at the time, I see it now. There was a support system that helped prop up our poor shattered family at that tragic time. The weekend my dad died was pretty much a blur. Once again I think of that protective blanket of shock. But I also remember that safe, soft world of my pillow, the haven I came back to every night after a long day of putting on a stoic front. I couldn't let on how I felt. I hid my grief, afraid to show the raw edge of my soul. But once I hit that refuge away from the world, I'd burrow my face into that private place of uncontrollable sobs, crying until I was empty, and could then drift off into oblivion. Recurring dreams were my constant companions for years following that mournful day. And in every dream, my father would say, "I haven't gone anywhere." Some of the dreams would involve secret government missions where my dad was not allowed to let on that he was still very much alive.

My dad was one of the few radicals interested in cryogenics back in the 60's. Apparently there was a big argument at the time of his death about whether or not to freeze him. Some family members argued it was what he wanted, and there was even a call put out to a center in Arizona. But in the end, a typical burial was chosen.

There was many a time, after hearing this information, that I'd felt upset they hadn't asked us, his children, how we felt about the subject. I would have welcomed the opportunity to give my input. My vote would have been to have him frozen.

I'm not sure how long my dreams continued, but at some point in my late teens they faded into that fortress of denial, where they would stay until I could better deal with them. Years passed, and that fortress was padded with more and more layers of protection. It became Castle Void, a subliminal, untouchable place, a black hole, holding a collapsed soul prisoner.

Marriage and kids were as good as mortar and stone to build those walls. And they were beautiful walls. The stone was of such fine quality, so sturdy, with a gleam and shine to it. Even after those walls fell in my mid 20's, when I finally faced my grief, some of the stones remained and they stand today like a Stonehenge around me, providing support and perspective.

The dreams about daddy didn't recur until I was thirty. Seven months pregnant with my fourth child, Adam, I'd gotten pneumonia and broke a rib during a coughing fit. (And no, I had the name picked out before that happened!) I was more uncomfortable than I could ever imagine. I couldn't even sleep in my bed, so I propped myself up on the couch, with the nice back support. I would drift off in fitful bouts of sleep, gazing at the wall covered with pictures of my three little girls, and a single picture of my dad. It was on one of these nights, lying there feeling lonelier and more helpless than at any other time in my adult life, that I had a final dream of my dad.

It was the same scenario as all the others. He was wearing that soft, dark green, flannel shirt that I so loved. He repeated the line he'd said so many times before, but with more conviction. "I haven't gone anywhere." In my disbelief, I said, "Hold on, I need to get my camera." And with a sigh and a slump of his shoulders he turned from me. Shaking his head, he walked away. I detected the slightest smile of resignation as he disappeared into a pathway of light.

I woke with a start. Unlike any other dream I'd had of him, I could feel his presence in that room. I could even smell that aroma of lingering cigars and earthiness he had about him.

That was the last time I saw him . . .

*****

I look ahead. The mirages on the road hover there, just out of touch, just out of reach, so like those dreams.

The sun climbs higher and so does the heat. I can feel my Yankee skin soak up these wonderful warm rays, storing them up to take home to what will be a long stretch of wearing many layers of clothing. I grow so weary of layering.

Appreciation also wells up in me, thinking how nice it is to be biking outside here. Pretty much from November to April any biking is done indoors on a trainer in Michigan. There are indeed those truly dedicated individuals who bike outdoors all year. There are a few out at the park where I train, who will be out there in the coldest and most brutal conditions. I've a great deal of respect for them, especially one fellow, Scott, a hand-cyclist. He lost the use of his legs in an accident many years ago. After an initial escape into drugs and alcohol, in which he gained more than three hundred pounds, Scott discovered hand-cycling. He is another at the top of my Hero list.

I'll be out there running along the path, padded with four layers of clothing on a wild winter day, and there ahead of me in the distance I'll see a figure in a bright neon-yellow jacket on the road. I know it's him. As I get closer to him, and I can see his amber goggles and his beet-red cheeks, a big white smile comes across his face. I'm filled with such admiration as I wave and smile back. If I had been grumbling and complaining to myself before, now I feel wimpy for even having thought it.

*****

At the pace I'm going, averaging 15 miles per hour, I should be able to finish this bike by about 3:30pm. And with the sun setting at 4:45, it doesn't give me a whole lot of light to run in.

I reach the 56-mile mark along highway 20 and see the many volunteers along the road in their matching tee shirts. As I approach, a couple of volunteers radio ahead to others that we're coming in to the midway checkpoint. They call our number out so the volunteers up ahead have our special needs bags ready by the time we get there. Such organization!

A volunteer holds out my bag as I ride up, but I wave and yell my "Thanks, but no thanks!" All I have in the bag is more food, a tire tube, a pair of socks in case it had been raining, and a shirt in the event of it getting chilly. Fat chance! I wish I could've stuck an air conditioner in there!

Halfway through this! Well, through the bike anyway. They say the "halfway point" in an ironman is at the 90-mile mark on the bike, even though the entire race is 140.2 miles long. Like a marathon, where they say the half way point is the last six miles of the 26.2 race, obviously it just means that last portion is that much harder. Once again, I have to stop thinking of the entire amount of miles I have to go today. 140.2 miles is like swimming, biking, and running to Toledo from Troy and back. Enough!

I make a right turn onto highway 231, happy to cross off another road on this journey. This highway business is getting to me! Only ten to twelve more miles on this road though.

Usually, I thoroughly enjoy driving along a highway, taking in the long expanses of landscape, the great stretches of sky, and listening to my favorite pieces of music. And I'm always counting hawks along the way. It's a great opportunity to focus on the journey, not the destination at the end. But there's a big difference between sitting in a car, and motoring the vehicle yourself!

Cranking away here, up down, up down, round and round my short legs go. The cadence and my breathing go hand in hand. I have my dad's legs, perfect for a gymnast, but not for a cyclist or runner. At five foot eight, he wasn't your long and lean type. But I've been told "he was a real looker." He had that buff and compact look to him, a Jack Lalanne type. He would've made a great triathlete. But he was gone long before the sport even came about.

I always thought he was the most handsome man on earth. When he was eighteen, he had sent away for the Charles Atlas (holder of the title, World's Most Perfectly Developed Man in the 1930's) body-building course. And apparently my dad was unhappy with his results. We have an old letter from Charles Atlas apologizing to my dad for his dissatisfaction with the program. Mr. Atlas also sent back a $20 check as a refund honoring the "guaranteed satisfaction" clause, stating that my dad was "one of the few who had not received wonderful results." When I look at the bulked up photo of Mr. Atlas on the letter, I can't help thinking, thank heavens it didn't work!

The first known triathlons were held in San Diego's Mission Bay in 1974. They began as light-hearted breaks from the training for marathons and 10ks.

John Collins, a U.S. Naval Officer, was instrumental in turning these carefree events into what is now known as Ironman. It was a challenge to others in the Armed Services.

Twelve men competed in the first race held in January 1978. In 1979, the first woman would compete as one of the 13 competitors. 1980 brought the first television coverage with the Hawaii Ironman on ABC's Wide World of Sport.

It was in those early 80's that I watched it for the first time on TV. I was fascinated by the concept, and entranced by the whole idea. Every year after that, I looked forward to watching Ironman, that intriguing sport. But never, never in those early years had it crossed my mind that it was something I might do.

*****

I come up on another turn onto Camp Flowers Road. Even just another turn on this long, flat route seems exciting, breaking up the monotony. Another road checked off!

Now I am traveling along a more populated area with farms and homes with some acreage. I see a few horses grazing contentedly with their tails swishing away. The smell of manure pacifies me with mixed feelings—happiness, and also a reminder of the hard work it was to own a horse and pony.

I got my pony, Shadow, the spring that we moved into our Edencroft home. He was one of the wild ponies of Chincoteague .

Our family had traveled to Chincoteague in the summer of 1964, and I fell in love with the ponies. We watched the famous wild pony roundup and pony crossing from Assateague island to Chincoteague.

I was traumatized when one of the news boats hit one of the ponies and it went under, drowning. They pulled it out and laid it on the shore. Everything inside me was crying out to run over to give the poor thing mouth to mouth resuscitation.

Why did they do nothing? I felt such an anger rising within me. Those STUPID news people! But I was only nine. So I did nothing, nothing but carry a sense of guilt for the rest of my life that I did nothing!

At that point in my life everything was about horses and ponies.

My dad would bring us gifts when he'd go on his business trips to give talks and lectures on the Space program. He'd always bring me either fancy molded plastic horses, or books filled with beautiful photographs of my favorite beasts, and information on how to take care of them. My dad and I worked together to "break" this wild creature, this grey pony with the white stripe down his nose. I named him after the Robert Louis Stevenson poem, "I Have a Little Shadow," and would recite parts of the poem as I rode along on his back.

I watched when the vet came to castrate my poor pony. Even though I was young enough to be naive about this domination of man over beast, I still felt a gnawing in my gut that there was something terribly wrong with this whole process.

I've often thought of myself as a wild creature and resent the idea of having to be captured, broken, and tamed. What is it in human nature, this need to capture and control that which God has designed? The Laws of Nature far outweigh any man-made laws. Why do we feel this need to put rules, regulations, and boundaries onto everything? Often I've found myself resisting such mortal-made mandates! Yes, I was the trouble-causing black sheep of the family, the rebel, but that's a story for another book!

Shadow was a rebel too. But I did enjoy working together with my dad to bring this creature around to our way of thinking. Shadow certainly did have a mind of his own, and managed to embarrass me numerous times with his defiance. I seemed to focus on that one line from the poem, "and can only make a fool of me in every sort of way" quite often in my riding recitations.

Shadow was not a good "show pony." He'd either suddenly stop and put his head down to throw me off, or back up when he didn't get his way—quite often at the most inopportune times. He'd just stop, and back up! And a few times, backing into bushes, he managed to knock me off. As he trotted off, I swear I could see a grin on his face, and a twinkle in his eye.

I guess I was secretly happy that we never did manage to break his spirit! But there was a day I decided to use reverse psychology on him. He started backing up and I kept him backing up in a circle for what seemed like an eternity. We backed around and around and around. I kept pulling on the bridle to keep him from moving forward. After that, I don't think he ever used that ploy again.

I'd also used reverse psychology on my horse, Senator, a couple of times. He was not as intelligent as Shadow, so it worked a lot better on him. He was a sweet horse, but he had been abused by a former owner so he didn't like men. He was a bit of a challenge for that reason, but he loved to chase down other riders or a deer. Those moments of gliding along with no effort on my part with the wind in my face, feeling the power of this animal underneath, felt so freeing.

I guess that was as close to biking as I cared to get back then.

*****

Biking along, I suddenly see a car up ahead traveling at a very slow speed. A hand emerges out the window with what looks like a chocolate bar. I realize it's my sisters in the rented car trying to entice me. Cathy sticks her head out calling,

"You're going to have to move a lot faster than that if you want this chocolate!" I laugh, knowing they're just teasing me. You really can't accept any outside help from anyone along the course. This is supposed to be done on your own!

My sisters drive off ahead. It was a brief but welcome distraction. Family dynamics are a funny thing, especially when you get to be adults. I got mixed reactions when I told my siblings and mom what I was going to be doing in this race. Mostly, I think they just thought I was nuts. But at least Jency and Cathy understood enough to come down and be a part of my adventure.

Once again, I'm pondering the whole idea myself. Why does someone do this race? Is it the challenge? Is it to see how far you can push yourself before you break? Is it to prove something? I'm hoping for that answer by the time I finish. I keep cranking away, wondering when I'll see my sisters again.

*****

Onto road 2301, "Check!" A little further up, I make a left onto highway 388. I'll have a bit of a stretch here, but the next turn will take me back onto highway 79. I can't wait. But once again, I am careful not to look too far ahead.

I did some research deciding to do this particular ironman race. There are about 20 different ironman races around the world. Hawaii is the only one you have to qualify for.

I chose Florida because it has the flattest bike course of any ironman race in the states. I figured if I'm biking 112 miles I'd like it to be flat. Some argue that with the hills you don't have to pedal as many miles with all those down hills. But to get to those down hills, I argue back, you have to bike up the hills first. It takes twice the energy for me to bike uphill, so it's not worth it.

Suddenly I realize the wind is picking up. This was something I dreaded, going into a head wind on the way back. It's almost as bad as a hill.

I've been on long group training rides where there will be a long line of us. I always seem to end up in the tail-end spot.

I dub myself "caboose," because I so rarely hold any other position. There have been times I've ended up crying, being hit with strong headwinds and losing the wheel ahead of me. It takes great concentration and some persistence to hang onto someone's wheel for long periods of time. Perhaps I don't have the attention span for it!

Once I've dropped off in that situation, it takes so much energy to try to catch back up, and it becomes so demoralizing when I can't quite reach them. I watch them fade away in the distance, trying to take comfort in the thought that in a triathlon this is the way it would be anyway, alone . . .

But that's the way I've experienced a lot of my years. All through my school years, and even in my marriage, surrounded by four children and a husband, I felt alone, not quite fitting in anywhere. It's always been the old square peg not fitting into the round hole.

According to some of the stories I've heard, my father experienced a similar isolation. He was the quiet, thoughtful type, so sensitive that his grandmother and mother worried about him from the start, insisting he needed special care. In his mind, brother Bill was the oldest, so he was lucky. Bob was the youngest, so he was lucky. Aubrey was the only girl, so she was lucky. That left him unlucky.

Even as his mother lay dying in 1959, she was still worrying about him, though he was 38 years old at the time.

Daddy struggled from the very start with school. Having a terrific imagination didn't help in the left-brained environment. He had to be taught simple tricks like "D" has a fat stomach, "B' has a double fat stomach in order to grasp the basics. From very early on he was very conscious and conscientious of every moment, and didn't wish to waste any time on what seemed unimportant to him. He wasn't interested in what others wanted him to learn. He was learning just fine on his own! He missed a lot of the "controlled" schooling, being absent a lot. This was yet another thing we had in common.

My report card at the end of fourth grade had a little note to my parents saying I'd missed over half my schooling to that point.

Yes, I was sick a lot, or maybe just sick of school a lot. I have a vivid recollection of a time I headed off to school from our Cherry Lane home. My brother, sister and I walked to school together, only living a quarter mile from school. But this day, really just not wanting to go to school, I told them I'd catch up, then promptly crawled behind a bush next to our house.

I sat for a period of time enjoying the underworld of that bush. There was something so peaceful about sitting under that canopy, hidden from the world in the quiet dark. The smell of the composting leaves and other debris and the occasional spiders aren't exactly what most would consider beautiful, but I did.

And when I felt it was a long enough chunk of time, long enough to be too late to go to school, I went back in the house and told my mom I didn't feel well enough to go to school. Little did she know how well I felt after sitting under that bush.

My poor mom. She had her hands full with my stubbornness when it came to not wanting to attend school. I tried all the tricks in the book when it came to pretending I was sick, including things like holding the thermometer against a light bulb. I remember a time in high school when, in her desperation to wake me up when I wouldn't get out of bed, Mom doused me with a cup of water in the face.

But I didn't "play hooky." It wasn't so much about playing. I didn't stay home to watch TV or play with dolls. I stayed home from school so I could learn by studying what interested me. I wanted to be the teacher! I loved reading about birds and animals, and I got more of an education being outside than I ever did in that structured world of learning.

I've always comforted myself with the fact that Edison and Einstein both dropped out after struggling with that confined learning environment. And though I'm no Einstein or Edison, my father got to hang around in one of their shadows, quite literally. When he was at Princeton, he did student work under Einstein.

When my dad was in sixth grade, he thought he had invented a ray gun, but when he related this to his father, who had a PhD in chemistry, he got a rather scornful reaction.

I wonder about my grandpa Cole and what he was like as a father. He was a chemist, and when they lived in Sandusky he worked for Crayola. My aunt fondly remembers testing out the crayons.

I've heard stories of how my grandfather invented "Freon" and a poison ivy lotion that closely resembled Calamine lotion, but somehow, because of his lack of business sense, didn't get the credit he deserved.

There has been a family joke that Goody Cole, our token witch in the ancestry, put a curse on the entire family line that none would be financially successful. Perhaps this is why my Grandfather Cole's inventions never made it "big"!

There was a story of a rocket my father built and demonstrated in eighth grade. He put out a constant stream of inventing, creating, thinking, yet still also kept up with physical interests. He was forever wrestling with brother Bill, and both played football on the Bryn Athyn eighth grade teams, so colorfully named, " Meat Grinders" and "Bone Crushers."

School was never in the forefront of Daddy's mind back then. He would much prefer hanging out at the Pennypack Creek playing on Three Kid Island or swinging on the ropes in the sycamore trees, leaving his mind free to create. I've been told he liked to swing through the trees with a knife in his teeth.

Dad's high school years were filled with summers of hitchhiking across the country, visiting and working for aunts, uncles all along the way, doing odd jobs like milking cows and delivering milk.

In the summer of 1938, he stayed with his Uncle Paul and Aunt V doing tree work with his good friend "Red." That was the summer he finally got his driver's license. It cost a whole quarter.

In July 1939, his last summer of high school, Daddy was accepted at Princeton, though older brother Bill would try to convince him to come join him at Harvard.

In the letter he wrote to his mother from Shepherdstown, West Virginia while visiting relatives, commenting on being accepted to Princeton, he didn't seem too enthusiastic. He stated, "But I don't know what the hell I want to do after school and what I'm going to prepare for in school."

It amazes me that he sounded so lost at that point. He always struck me as someone who knew exactly what he wanted in life. But I guess we all have our times of stumbling around, looking for that destiny that sits right under our noses.

But Daddy would find his purpose, in looking to and writing about a future that few could even fathom. He was singled out often for his unusual ideas.

"As early as 1953, before the U.S. even had a space program, he predicted a manned moon landing by 1970." (Quoted from Wikipedia, citing a 1964 article in Fortune Magazine)

He was a strong individualist. Fortune Magazine (August 1964) would say, "Cole's ideas about the future emerge as wild as bees." Further in, the article stated that Dad's ideas were too bizarre to worry much about at the time, but the gradually growing consensus that it was "less dangerous to listen to things fantastic than it [was] to ridicule them."

I guess things like living in hollowed out asteroids, landing on the moon, and being frozen at the time of death were just not a part of every day average thought in the 50's and early 60's.

*****

At the 90-mile point, the headwinds become quite strong and I start feeling very discouraged, especially thinking this is only the halfway point of the race. I can't think like that! Too much thinking. I can't help picturing Winnie the Pooh, saying "Think, think, think," whereas, when he was trying hard to think more, I spend a lot of time wishing I could do less.

I remember one of the boot camp letters my dad wrote to his sister, trying to reassure her when she was struggling at Bryn Mawr college. He was speaking of one of his boot camp buddies, Woo, a young Chinese artist who "doesn't think too quickly" but "that is just a matter of relativity." He went on, "You could think at the speed of one word per hour and still do more useful thinking in your life than anyone else on earth— provided that your thinking was sufficiently accurate, clear, and intuitive."

I try not to think. I sing to myself, but all that comes out of my mouth are words to songs like "The Long and Winding Road" by John Lennon and "Walk Down that Lonesome Road" sung by James Taylor. No, this definitely isn't helping.

I come up to the left turn back onto highway 79. Yes! Finally now I am feeling a little more energy. With only 12 more miles to go, the last leg of this torturous part of the journey doesn't seem so bad. And though it's a flat course, this now feels like a downhill. I am able to smile again.

The last twelve miles breeze by, something I never would have guessed. I don't know that anything has ever felt so satisfying than to finish these last miles. This has been a journey, though I know I'm in store for still another in the next hours of my day.

I think of this long journey and wonder, is this how the Israelites felt wandering in the wilderness for 40 years? Did they know when they were getting toward the end? Perhaps this is a good analogy of my life since my childhood, wandering through the wilderness looking for answers, wondering what the purpose is.

I turn left onto Back Beach Road, nearly almost there now, so close I can almost taste it.

As I head into the transition area, thick crowds are everywhere. The cheering and the announcer's voice commingle with the heavy humid air. I hear the song "Who Let the Dogs Out" and smile, shaking my head at the ridiculous lyrics that have become so popular.

I come to the dismount line, worried whether I'll be able to even stand when I get off. It's been hours since my feet have touched the ground.

I unclip, and my tired hands clench on the brakes. I feel it in my upper arms, so tired from holding me up all those hours. I tried to relax while I rode, but a certain amount of tension is unavoidable. I swing my right leg over the back, unbelievably happy I can let go of this mode of transport, hearing the cheers, the "Good job!"s and "Way to go!"s.

I hand off my bike to the nearest volunteer yelling, "You can throw that thing in the ocean for all I care. I never want to see it again!" Some of the spectators laugh. And with a big smile on her face the volunteer yells back, "You'd be surprised how many people are saying that today!"

I run (if you can call it that!) up to the racks, looking for my number, grab my bright orange 'bike to run' bag and head to the tent. I am so thankful to have made it through that most difficult part of the race.

There is a part of me that can't believe I biked that far. Once again I think if someone had told me, even two or three years ago, that I'd be able to bike 112 miles, especially after swimming 2.4 miles, I would have to say they were nuts! That's just not possible, is it? Can a 45-year-old mother of four, soon to be a grandma, really be doing this? It's just not believable. And yet here I am doing it. And I'm actually even enjoying some of it!

Onward! The day is young.

Chapter Five:
T-2

"You can't predict the future, but you can invent it."
—Dandridge MacFarlan Cole

This second transition is a lot tougher than the visit to the tent seven hours ago. Did I really just spend seven hours sitting on that bike seat!? I'm still having a hard time comprehending it.

My legs feel like blocks of wood, two-by-fours, dry and stiff. I wobble as if I'm walking on stilts.

I come into the tent amidst a lot of women. Yes, this time it's very different. I had about 1200 people pass me on the bike and it seems like a good portion of them are in here right now! But realistically, I know there is usually a female-to-male ratio of 25 percent to 75 percent, so I know there really aren't that many women in here. It just seems like it.

I change into my running shorts, welcoming the freed feeling of getting out of spandex. I put on my running shoes, tying them loosely with a little room for expansion, and double bow them to keep them from coming undone. Some call it "having a flat tire" when you're running and the laces come undone. In one race I did, they not only came undone, but the one shoe went flying up behind me as I was coming into the finish line. I guess you could've called that a "blow out." I was not going to stop to pick it up and let someone pass me, not after having already stopped to tie it a quarter mile before. One of the finish line photos actually showed the shoe in the air. An excited spectator gladly brought me my sweaty lost "tire" after I crossed.

*****

I sit. I sigh. But it's time to move on. It was a brief but wonderful moment of sitting. I top myself off with the Timex cap from my bag, and I'm off to face this new challenge of staying upright for another minimum of four hours!

I run out of the tent, once again being asked if I want suntan lotion. Once again I say "No thanks," but want to add, "Look, we really only have about one hour of daylight left here. Who needs suntan lotion?" I guess one can get kind of crabby and ungrateful at times during these races. Apologies to you all!

*****

I've done races where I've thought how nice it would be to have my dad there, cheering me on. He would've been there, just as he would've been there for all the big transitions in my life.

Dad would have been there at my high school graduation, probably with that movie camera in his hand. He loved that thing. He took movies of us from the days in Colorado, at the pool and filming our antics on the trampoline at home, all of us taking turns jumping, jumping. There was also a clip of us swinging on ropes into our big sand pile.

We had an acre lot in Denver, with big pine trees surrounding it. My dad strung ropes from the trees, and we'd get a new truck-load of sand each year dumped into a spot right off our patio to swing into. Imagine having a parent that was still kid enough to want a sand pile, but on a huge scale. And he'd play in it with us! I loved the feel and smell of the big thick ropes, of hanging on tightly with the wind blowing through my hair as I swung. And I loved the drop into the soft, cool sand.

Daddy also started building an elaborate tree house in between four of the sap-filled giants. We moved before he could finish that project.

There were some sedate movie clips of us dressed in our Easter best before going off to church in Denver, posing in front of the wall outside our front door. With we three girls in bonnets and gloves and my brothers in bow ties, we looked like a perfect little 1950's family.

We were part of a small Swedenborgian church group there in Colorado. One of my few recollections about church was the big great Dane named 'Denver' that the minister and his family owned. When we'd visit their home after church, that dog would come bounding up like some giant behemoth and snag my mother's stockings and slobber all over us. And though it seemed a bit overwhelming at the time, these giant creatures have always intrigued me.

In our livingroom we had a big 12" by 24" heat grate we'd sit on. Two of us could fit on it at once. And for the most part it was a comfy, cozy place. But there was a time after a visit to church that I was thinking about the biblical characters

Shadrack, Meschack, and Abednego burning in the fiery fur-
nace, and I worried about suffering the same fate sitting on
that heat grate. These are my recollections of religion in Colorado. It's funny how a kid's imagination works.

There were recorded trips to the seashore in the 60's.
There's a clip of me in the blue shore house with a room full
of monarch butterflies, and even a shot of one perched on my
nose, opening and closing its wings, while I watched this wonder of nature cross-eyed. I must have discovered a bunch of
them enroute in their migration to Mexico. I have no idea how
I managed to catch a whole roomful, and I can't believe my
mom and dad let me do it. But there it is, a magical segment
of my life caught on film.

The movie then pans to my brother Steve and his collection
of star fish. He holds one in each hand, and shows a display
spread out across the picnic table on the deck, plus a full shop-
ping bag. One has to wonder if these recorded events didn't
push the entire populations of star fish and monarch butterflies
to the brink of extinction.

That camera followed us everywhere, with my father close
behind.

I remember wishing I could have introduced him to my
first love, the man I would marry. Daddy certainly would've
been there for my wedding in August of 1975. Even though it
was not a tradition in our church to have the dad give away
the bride, I like to picture it happening that way.

I guess that's the beauty in dreaming of events that
couldn't happen. I can create the whole picture the way I want
it. I do remember my wedding as a time I really did feel a tug
on my heart because he wasn't there. But in my mind I see
him there all the same, his camera in hand, strolling around

the Cathedral grounds.

When I had my first child, Norah, I could imagine him filming or holding her. I named her after the babysitter we had when we were down at the shore.

My dad and mom hired this 16-year-old blonde beauty named Norah Ingersoll to watch us. She looked Scandinavian but I'm not sure if she was. She had that sun-kissed look, and we just adored her. She must have appreciated the connection, because she was there at my dad's funeral that October in 1965.

With each child I had, it was a time to really miss that bond I could have had with my dad if he had been alive. I can picture him looking down into the crib of any one of my four babies and smiling tenderly, singing them a lullaby. He wrote and published a lullaby for my youngest sister, Mary Jane. I can still hear him singing it or whistling it, " Oh Janey, My Baby." It had a Celtic feel to it. Originally he'd written the song back at boot camp as "Bonnie Wee Jamey" for his brother who died at birth, but changed the lyrics to suit his last little treasure.

I wonder if he would say the same thing about one of my babies that he said of me when I lay in my crib at eight weeks old. He leaned over me and declared to my mother's sister Katie, "She is the most knowing baby I've ever seen." When I picture Daddy with a grandchild curled up in his lap, reading to them, telling them a great tale, I feel such a sadness that the tears still well up after all these years. I would have loved to see my dad with my children, to see that nurturing love showered down upon another generation, spilling forth like some waterfall from the river of family love.

So many transitions of my life have gone by with a gaping hole, with that "something" missing.

I think of those smiles in the home movies, so innocent, so unknowing of the future. I ache for the child behind those smiles, so trusting that life will continue just as it had with the security of two parents, in a world filled with fun and adventure.

Sometimes life can be so painful. One wonders how and why we continue. These endurance races are such a perfect metaphor for our lives. To push through the struggle, the pain, the tragedy, to the edge (and sometimes beyond) of breaking, to look to that inner strength, that power beyond our own, only makes us stronger.

As I grow older and wiser, I understand more fully that everything happens for a reason. Often, I can even look back and see the purpose behind an event that at the time didn't make sense. But I must confess that I still can't see the reason behind the tragedy of losing this person in my life. I understand and trust that there is a reason far beyond my comprehension, and someday I hope to see it in the grand scheme of things.

Life is such a puzzle. Many times I see myself finding a piece, adding it to the big picture. I love puzzles! And I love finally discovering a segment I've been searching for and putting it into place. Perhaps this is a piece that will take a lifetime to find. Perhaps it's the final piece. And as much as I love finding the parts and putting them together, there is a sadness in completing it. So I hope to hold off finding that last piece until I've lived a good long life.

Did my father find that last piece to his puzzle too early on?

Chapter Six:
The Run

"What of the dreams of today? With enormous enlargement of our horizons that has taken place in the last fifty years, these dreams can be truly breathtaking. Many of these dreams will be the reasonable hopes of tomorrow. Beyond tomorrow they will become realities."
—Dandridge M Cole, ***Beyond Tomorrow*** (1965)

The marathon is a crazy beast. And before you put the saddle on, you have to know what this creature will do to you.

I wouldn't know what this meant going into my ironman race, it's only in the years following that I would understand. And having no clue going into it was probably better. If I'd done a marathon first, it probably would have convinced me to re-think this pursuit.

A marathon is a specific distance in running, 26.2 miles. The marathon was originally conceived as a race for the 1896 Olympics in Athens, then transported to Boston in 1897.

The original 24.85 mile distance was inspired by the legend of the Greek soldier, Pheidippides, a messenger sent from the Battle of Marathon in 490 B.C. to Athens, where he announced that the Greeks had beaten the Persians in battle.

The story goes that he ran the entire distance without stopping, burst into the assembly exclaiming "Nenikekamen" (We have won!), before collapsing and dying.

There is debate over the historical accuracy of the legend though.

The actual 26.2 miles (42.195 kilometers) wasn't established until the 1908 Olympic Marathon in London. They set the 26 mile distance to cover the ground from Windsor Castle to White City Stadium with the 385 yards added so the race could finish in front of King Edward VII's royal box. But it took 16 years of heated debate before the distance became official at the 1924 Olympics in Paris.

*****

Before I attempted this goal of Ironman, I'd hoped to at least have one marathon under my belt. But the first marathon I signed up for this past February was just not meant to be. I got a stress fracture in my lower leg just weeks before the race, and had to stop running altogether for two months. And I wondered if I should even drop out of the ironman though it was still nine months away.

But my friend Ray, who'd done his share of Ironman races, said, "Nah, don't worry about it. You can always walk the marathon. You just need to be able to bike 112 miles, because you can't walk that!" His reassurance was enough, and a good dose of naivete' helped too.

*****

So here I am, at the beginning of my very first marathon, not knowing what to expect. The longest race I've done is an Olympic distance triathlon with only a six mile run. The entire race took me three hours to finish. And in training, the longest I'd gone was an 80 mile bike with a six mile run, totaling six hours. Six hours! Ironman will be two or three times that! I try not to think of it.

I head out of the transition area to the rousing cheers of all the spectators. Those rousing cheers are what get us through this, a life force sometimes greater than food or drink. Taking a quick right onto S. Thomas Drive I commence my journey on foot.

I've changed into nice dry running shorts, but I can't say I'm feeling like a new woman. I'm feeling stiff and old, yet still excited that I am here taking part in a dream. I wish I could say I feel like I'm floating along in a dreamlike state, but this is reality, as tough as reality gets. The thump, thump, clump, clump of my feet will be the music I hear for hours to come.

I took up running only five years ago. When I turned forty, my metabolism changed, and for the first time in my life I started to really put on weight. I think I gained about ten pounds before I realized that the swimming wasn't doing the trick.

So I started watching fat grams and calories. Having never done this in 40 years of life, it wasn't easy. And as much as I'm disciplined in exercising, I'm not in my eating habits. I had to do something different. So I took up running instead.

When I swim, I burn about 400 calories, when I bike 500, but when I run I burn a good 600 calories or more, depending on my pace. There's no question about it, running is the way to get the best calorie burning workout, especially when limited with time. It's the "best bang for your buck".

In all my life before age 40, I'd never run more than 15 to 20 minutes, and that 15 to 20 minutes was grueling. I never understood what people saw in running. But those first minutes, when you're getting your heart rate up, are the toughest. It's only after you get past that initial period that it gets easier.

I started running 30-45 minute stints at the Bally's club on the track three or four times a week, plus swimming every day. One day a young fellow, Ken, caught me in the pool and suggested I try a triathlon. I looked at him with a skeptical tilt of my head and said, "You mean like Ironman?" He said "No, there are shorter distance triathlons, baby triathlons."

This guy had not one ounce of fat on him, and I asked him what kind of diet he ate. When he said the "See food diet" I asked "sea food, like fish?" He said "No, I see food, I eat it." I didn't need to hear anymore. I knew I'd like this new training regime. He became my mentor. Once again I think of that quote about people coming into your life for a reason.

*****

My plan is to run through the miles, and then walk through the aid stations situated at each mile mark. It will give me a little break, and enough time to grab the fluid and food I need to survive this thing.

I finished my bike by 3:30pm and I've only got an hour and a half of daylight left. This will be my first race in the dark.

About 15 minutes into my run I see the lead male athlete, Jamie Cleveland, coming in for what would be an 8:37:58 finish. Imagine! I'm just beginning my run here, and he's finishing his race. Alec Rukosuev runs past in second place and finishes with an 8:46:14. They were almost twice as fast as I was on the bike!

114

An hour later Tara-Lee Marshall would finish as first woman in 9:33:49. Somehow I missed seeing her, probably too engrossed in keeping a steady pace going.

It's an honor to be a part of a race with such phenomenal athletes. And as much awe and respect I have for those pros that win this thing, I have equal, if not more respect for those pros that, due to injury or hitting the wall, struggle through the rest of the race with us age-groupers. Some pros just drop out when they know they can't come in the top money-making slots. But there are those commendable elites that tough it out, follow through, and finish. That's what it's really about—the perseverance, not the money!

You learn a lot about yourself in endurance racing. You learn that you have more strength than you thought possible. "Mind over matter", or as William Paley states in Natural Theology (1802), "The essential superiority of spirit over matter."

The mind is a powerful thing. Once again I'm picturing one of the illustrations in my father's book, Beyond Tomorrow.

Entitled "Saucer Men," it's a black and white drawing of three saucers with just the bald head of a man in a glass dome in each one. Mechanical arms extend from their disc-like bodies. This was the picture I was most drawn to (other than the undersea laboratory). Looking at it, I felt a mixture of fascination and being a little "creeped out" by this depiction of man without a body.

It's a part of the chapter entitled "Improvements In Man" which was an interesting look into the future of man from this scientist's perspective. In this chapter my father reflects, in a discussion about all the modern improvements to health such as "corrective eye lenses rather than corrective exercises...", and organ and artificial transplants, he reflects that perhaps we are taking the "easy way" out. He reasons that "...to endure pain, hardship, and even risk loss of a certain percentage of the race to environmental extremes, disease, etc. while the natural bodily and evolutionary processes strengthen the individual and the race.

The gorilla and the dolphin chose this course. To a great extent the Australian bushman and the Kurds of Persia did also. But most of the race in its cowardly, lazy, pleasure-seeking fashion has tried constantly to reduce exposure to pain, danger, hardship, discomfort, and labor, and to increase security and pleasure. This tendency to use his brain and hands to manipulate his environment and thus to decrease danger and discomfort and increase security and pleasure is perhaps the most characteristic behavior of homo sapiens. It has led him to the point where total control over the environment is within sight, but it has also led to weakening of the individual and the race."

I think about this in terms of athletes that strive to achieve their goals. We are certainly throwing ourselves into "pain, danger, hardship, discomfort, and labor" and all to strengthen and improve our person. I wonder if there isn't in this some deep-seated hope of improving the overall race. When an individual is inspired by watching an athlete, not unlike my interest in watching Ironman on TV, it can drive them to get up off the couch and join the ranks of the "Doers", which of course can only strengthen the human race.

I think of a drop of water or stone hitting the surface of a lake or pool and the concentric circles that emanate out from it, or any of the concentric circles that ripple through nature with the wind or movement of any kind. Every move we make, every action we take, has that ripple effect. And we should strive to make that a positive ripple, affecting all those around us.

*****

I slow down to a walk going through an aid station. I take a cup of pretzels and at the end of the row of tables see a couple of garbage cans full of ice water and sponges. You can't imagine how good an icy cold sponge feels on a day like today.

I've seen runners with their sponges tucked into their shirts, under the straps of their singlets, and even stuffed under their caps. I've tucked ice cubes in my hat before. The ice melting and trickling down my head feels so refreshing on a hot day. Quite often on oppressive days the spectators will be kind enough to run a hose and spray us as we run by.

After weaving in and out of the streets on different little turns here and there, I get back onto S. Thomas Drive along the shoreline. I look out onto the Gulf and wonder once again why I am not lying on that beach out there. We are at the shore, in November! Why am I running all these miles when I could be relaxing on the nice white sand?

But then I turn my attention to all the faces of different runners. These are people I may have passed, or may have been passed by in the water or out there on the highways. I wonder about each of their stories. What led them here to this race? What obstacles did they face?

I see another Michigander named Roman, a tall, handsome, bearded fellow with long hair, striking in looks and name. I've seen him at some of the triathlons back home. I wave and say, "Go Michigan!"

He looks at me strangely, not knowing who the heck I am. I don't care. I'm just so excited to see someone else from my state.

I had looked at the participant list before coming down to see if I knew any of the other Michiganders aside from my friends. The list has pertinent information like age, city and state, and also occupation. It's fascinating to see the different occupations of people who attempt this challenge. There are students, attorneys, nurses, doctors, physical therapists, home-makers, all sorts of military, bankers, teachers, pumpkin farm-ers, landscapers and engineers, a real cross section of professions.

I also checked to see how many women are in my age group. How many other women my age are dealing with their "mid-life crisis" in this way? There are twenty listed for today's race.

I approach the condo, Moonspinner, that my friend Rod and my sisters and I are staying at. There's a small part of me that would like to cut off this course and go sit in that hot tub on the beach side of the condo. My sisters are there in front of the condo, standing along the road cheering with a handful of other spectators. Cathy comes running up with a water gun and starts shooting at me. I welcome the spray, but tell her she better spray the other participants so I won't get disqualified for having special attention in the race. I head left into St An-drew's Park.

I had done a short run into the park to check it out the other day with Rod, another Michigander hoping to survive his first Ironman.

I'm so impressed with Rod. He's taken on this challenge having just started swimming at the beginning of this year. I've heard that swimming is the most difficult discipline to add on, as the biking and running you can get by with not really mas-tering technique. He spent hours at the lake in Troy working on his swim technique.

The park is a beautiful 1,260 acre swath of land with over one and a half miles of beach on the Gulf and Grand Lagoon. It's the perfect picture of a Florida landscape; the dunes covered with quaking oat grass against the white sand. The park is alive with great blue herons, snowy egrets, laughing gulls, brown pelicans, and the smaller killdeers, red-winged black birds and numerous other common birds. Black swallowtails flit here and there on puffs of wind.

Across the ship's channel is Shell Island. It's a wild and pristine looking place, beckoning to me, calling to me. I kind of wish I'd planned my stay to extend a week after the race to enjoy the area.

I catch myself smiling, thinking about what the race director told us yesterday. "Whatever you do, don't go off in the shrubs or trees to do your business once you get into the Park, especially after dark. An alligator could grab you." I wondered if he said that to just scare us, or if there really have been any alligator attacks during a race.

As I run the loop around the beautiful Park, I am enjoying the wilderness though the air is heavy with humidity and my lungs are starting to ache (such a reminder to those Philadelphia summer days of my youth.)

I wonder if I will see my friends around the loop. Deb and Rod should both be coming up on me as their biking skills, like Chris's, are far better than mine. It's only a matter of time.

Chris and Deb tried to convince me to stay in the condos near all the action. But I ended up convincing Rod that this condo would be the place to stay. I know myself, and I need to be able to pull away from all the excitement around the Expo and transition area.

I recharge in quiet and peaceful surroundings. Yes, I love the condo we're staying at. It's the last condo along the beach across from the Park entrance.

In every place I've ever lived, there was always a "surrounded by nature" feel to it. There was only one brief year when I was first married that my husband and I lived in an apartment. I couldn't believe how much I hated living in that apartment. I felt so closed in, so claustrophobic. Insanity would've gotten me if it had gone on much longer than a year.

I ached to get my hands in the dirt. I ached beyond anything I could explain to those around me—my husband, his family, the people I knew through church. How could I describe this wild part of me without them thinking I was nuts?

Thankfully, my husband and I found a home with an acre lot and five acres of woods surrounding it by the end of our year contract with the apartment. And we were able to raise our children in the same environment I was accustomed to, cradled in the hands of nature.

I think of some of the wonderful settings I've trained in this year, places so beautiful. They seem even more beautiful to me once I've run, biked or swum through them. There's something so powerful about experiencing nature in an aerobic state. It heightens the experience, and adds so much. It almost gives me a sense of ownership, an intimacy and connectedness I'd never get driving through it. I become a part of it, and it becomes a part of me—a symbiosis.

One of the most memorable training moments I had was this past summer. I was at a summer camp with my kids in the Laurel Highlands around Somerset, Pennsylvania. It was a family church camp and there were about a hundred people attending.

I announced at one of the gatherings that I was going to be doing some training and asked if anyone wanted to join me. I found only two other guys interested in waking up at the crack of dawn to get in a run or swim before the day's full plan of activities. On this particular morning, I wanted to do a three mile run ending at the lake for a swim, and could only talk one of them, Calvin, into the adventure.

We headed out at 6:00am onto the hilly course, winding up and down the road through the park. It was such a beautiful area, the woods filled with wild flowers and carpeted with moss, the soft sounds of the birds echoing through the morning air.

But the run was just the debut, the first act in what would be the most unforgettable of swims. We ran down to the water's edge, kicked off our shoes, and I peeled off the tank top and shorts I'd been wearing over my swim suit. I put on the goggles I'd tucked into my shorts and hurried down to the cool lake before we'd had a chance to cool down from the run, and before we could think of any excuses why we shouldn't be getting in there.

The lake was absolutely magical. There was a thick layer of fog blanketing the entire body of water. The water was smooth and glasslike, but fading into the fog with no distinctive line dividing the two. Not wanting to break the beautiful silence of the area I spoke quietly, "We should probably stick together so as not to lose each other." I wasn't familiar with the lake so there was just a touch of apprehension. But I also felt an excitement to venture into such an ethereal-looking realm.

There is something so gratifying in being the first to break the smooth surface of water. It's like sticking the first spoon or knife into a jar of peanut butter. I wonder sometimes, what it is that makes that moment so rewarding? Is it my need to be the first? Or is it just that feeling of control or power to change? Whatever it is, I like it.

We broke that beautiful, smooth surface, and "dug in."

My strokes were hurried at first to get a little warmth into my body, but very quickly became nice and easy. We headed out into the center, then turned to swim down the length. All I could see was the soft white air melding into the water and Calvin not far from me, lifting arms up—in and out with each stroke.

In between strokes I was suddenly hearing music. Music? It's 6:30 in the morning and we're out in the middle of a rather large forested area. How can there be music? Where was it coming from?

I stopped. Calvin stopped to see why I'd stopped. He asked, "What's wrong?"

I said, "Don't you hear that?"

"Yeah, what is it?"

I couldn't believe it. It was so beautiful, classical music! Here we were in the middle of a foggy lake at the crack of dawn listening to classical music.

It was one of those moments you wish you could just capture and keep in a jar, unreal and dreamlike. I wished I could've stayed there soaking it in, but I was getting a chill not moving. So we continued on for about twenty minutes.

After getting out and getting back into our shoes and clothes, Calvin and I headed back up to the camp. But all the while I couldn't get out of my head what we had just experienced. It was one of those times I know I'll probably never repeat.

I've had other moments of swimming through fog-covered lakes, but none that could top that one.

*****

Right now I can only dream of swimming across a cool, foggy lake, but no such luck! It's humid and the air feels heavier than water. I head out of the Park and then back out onto S. Thomas Drive.

Once again there are my sisters, seeming to be having way too much fun. They're chatting with people that are sitting there, sharing that bond of "spectatorship" not unlike the bond we athletes experience. They all cheer as I pass.

The cheering boosts my less than enthusiastic gait, giving me a surge of energy. There have been times where I'm struggling along in a race, then decide, the heck with it, I feel like crap but I'm going to smile anyway!

I look at the spectators, watching us trudging along with grimaces on our faces, looking like we're dying, and I think, why in the world would they ever want to attempt this if we look so miserable? So I smile instead. And oh, what a reaction I get from the spectators. I hear, " Look, she's still smiling!" Right away that feeds me their energy. It's a give and take. I love those spectators!

The day draws to its close. Residents along the way are starting to have cookouts in their front yards as they cheer us on. The smell of barbecues normally would entice me, but when I'm running, it is one of the few times I'm not interested in eating.

At one of the homes, the music is playing loudly and they are a rowdy bunch. They offer runners beer and hot dogs. Hot dogs! I can't imagine anything more likely to upset my now very fragile digestive system.

At a couple of the aid stations, I've accepted cups of chicken broth, a good salt source. But it's getting harder to assimilate anything now. My body's not really interested in this thing called digestion. The key to surviving a race like Ironman is fueling. Being able to take in the nourishment and fluids is essential to your survival.

One of the tricks I've learned in the long hours of training, is to make use of every moment. Sometimes after a long run or bike I'm starving, but I also can't wait to climb into a tub full of hot water. So I've become rather fond of eating in the tub. Decadent, yes, but oh so satisfying after a long workout.

I also learned the fine art of the "cat nap." Whenever, or wherever I am, if I have a fifteen minute chunk of time, I can fall into a "snooze" as quickly as I can close my eyes. I've had moments where I'm in the Park parking lot where I train, waiting to meet a friend to bike or run with, and I'll drift off. After the brief doze I wake refreshed and ready for action.

*****

I see a hawk soaring with the wind, circling as the day winds down. As 5:00pm approaches, the sky starts pulling up its cover of night. The earth slips into the gentle arms of twilight. I run along, soaking up the sweet evening air.

I catch the scent of a cigar, probably some spectator enjoying the balmy night as they watch us ramble along . As much as I don't enjoy smelling cigar or cigarette smoke as I run, I can't help thinking of my first and last cigar.

I was nine years old. I was a tiny, quiet girl who so looked forward at night to the time my dad would return from work, sometimes at a late hour.

On this particular night he'd returned home late after dinner, and we kids were already bathed and ready for bed. I remember sitting in my flannel pajamas on the stairs in our home at the end of Cherry Lane, the place I so often perched, watching from between the posts of the banister as my dad sat to eat his late dinner. The staircase led down from the upstairs bedrooms, where I was supposed to be tucked in my bed for the night.

Daddy was having his favorite, liver and onions. As meals go with children, liver is not exactly a welcomed choice. But because on nights such as this where my father would motion me with his finger to come and join him and share his most treasured liver, it became a preference that went well into my adult years.

Now, when I think of liver, its odd texture and strong flavor, and its function as an organ that secretes bile, it doesn't exactly leave my mouth watering. But when I think of its use to produce that good, rich blood, that fluid that gives us life, and the good, rich memories of a meal shared with one you love, suddenly it becomes ambrosia of the gods.

We shared this treasured moment, and then my dad finished his meal with a bowl of Breyers Butter Almond ice cream, once again including me.

It was his custom to top off the meal with his cigar. Looking back, I can't help thinking that this was a perfect pattern for developing heart disease.

That night as he sat back and lit up his cigar, this little girl that so adored her father and wanted to emulate his every move asked to "take a puff" of his cherished smoke.

Daddy looked at me with those thoughtful brown eyes, and the twinkle rose up in them and he said, "Only if you smoke the whole thing." Always ready to rise to any challenge my father presented, I accepted the invitation, and proceeded to become sicker than I ever could've imagined at the hands of someone who cared so deeply for me. I didn't even make it to the halfway point before I ran off to the bathroom. Once again, had I not learned a huge lesson, I would have thought his methods verging on cruelty. But it worked. And I've never even so much as thought about taking a puff off anyone's cigar again!

Though Daddy had this bad habit of smoking cigars, he was careful to never promote the action. He'd been offered a chance to do a series of commercials for a well known cigarette company which could have brought him a nice four figure sum of money and national exposure, but he refused because he didn't want to encourage anyone, particularly teens, to smoke. I can't help wondering how tough that must have been for him to watch me get sick, even if it was a good lesson.

There seem to be many times where his loving hands were there in moments of sickness. In Colorado, when four of us came down with chicken pox, he fed us teaspoons of vodka and orange juice, now a method maybe not so popular, but it sure seemed to work at the time. I remember the outbreak as kind of fun!

And there was the time I swallowed a jack when I was four.

I was lying on my back on the carpet of our Denver living room floor watching TV with the little metal star-shaped game piece in my mouth, and suddenly it was lodged in my throat. As my dad scrambled to take me to the doctor's, I was more concerned and embarrassed about the bathing suit I was wearing. It was my sister's suit and it was pink, and I didn't even like pink.

The first doctor we went to was puzzled. When my dad

said I'd swallowed a jack, this professional, who we're supposed to entrust our lives with said, "You mean a card?" I was thankful that we moved on to another doctor. Our family doctor didn't know what to do either, so he sent us on to the hospital emergency

I remember sitting in the hallway on a guerney, still mortified that I was only wearing a pink bathing suit. The jack didn't hurt, but it was lodged in my throat none-the-less.

There was a nurse's aid, or perhaps she was a nurse, but she was wearing a nun's habit. I remember thinking, well, I may be dressed ridiculously, but at least I'm not wearing a hat with wings sticking out the sides! It looked to me like this woman could fall from a plane and successfully land. I was only four at the time, but somehow these things seemed important!

Eventually I was given a shot in preparation for surgery. Painful, but with the strong, supportive arm of my father around my shoulders, I felt safe. And shortly after that, I threw up. And not having the proper receptacle to puke into, my father held out his hands. And into those loving hands, I spilled the contents of my stomach.

The jack came out, and I was free to go. And as we left, I promised myself never to be caught dead out in public in a swim suit again.

Funny, here I am, now participating in a sport that quite often has me doing just that, running around publicly in just a swimsuit. Perhaps my childhood humiliation is one of the reasons I chose to change for the bike and run portions of this particular race.

And as I run down the road, the smell of the cigar fades into the distance along with all those warm images of my comforting caretaker. Who, with his medical training background, ended up creating an emergency tracheotomy kit in a sterile plastic case with a scalpel and plastic tube just in case something like this were to ever happen again.

He always was ahead of the times!

*****

I never grow weary of watching Nature's changing of the guards in the morning and in the evening.

Sunrise! Could there be a better time? With the morning's first light the bird's songs, bright and cheery, welcome the promise and potential of the day. It never ceases to fill me with joy and excitement watching the cresting of the sun on the horizon, one of the few moments we can look this ball of fire squarely in the eye and not go blind.

Then after a day of holding us all in the arms of its gravitational pull, the magnificent flaming giant slips back down to kiss the edge of the earth.

The evening bids a farewell and "good job" to all accomplishments achieved. The robins start their evening noises. Unlike their daytime songs, the chirps sound more like alarm calls. Are they as "alarmed" to lose their day as I am? Then the cardinals join in with their melodious farewells to the light.

Finally the chorus of crickets and cicadas that fill the airwaves of summer nights surround me and signal the end of evening rituals. It's time to unwind, to sit back and curl up into a comfortable position...or to run into the open arms of this friend, the night.

I've had plenty of training runs that took me into the dark. The park I run at is a great place for that. With its six mile loop around a lake, it's a safe spot to run. The asphalt path is nice and smooth, there are plenty of other runners, and the rangers are very good about keeping an eye on us.

I've had numerous friends caution me about the safety of such practices, but really there's very little danger. It's a whole lot safer than running along the roads after dark, and I love running in the dark. I try to reassure them saying, "If God didn't want me running in the dark, why would it be the powerful experience it is? Why would I feel so close to Him if I wasn't meant to be out there?"

If that doesn't work I just tell them I carry a tazer or stun gun. What's that African proverb?... "to run softly and carry a big stick"? Okay, it's really "Speak softly and carry a big stick," but I like my version.

When training I wear soft, quiet clothing, not the "swishy" sounding fabric that some jackets and wind pants and other "running clothing" are made of. I wear silent fabrics so that all I hear is my breathing and the soft clump, clump of my feet leaving me free to pick up the sounds of the turkeys roosting in the trees for the night, or the owls squawking and hooting, or sometimes the distant bark or howl of a coyote. I've even debated about wearing moccasins or going barefoot to mute my steps, but my friends already think I'm a little nutty as it is, so I'll stick to running shoes.

My running companions are Orion, The Big Dipper, Cassiopeia, Perseus, and the numerous other constellations that appear through the fall, winter and early spring. It's one of the few things I like about not having as many hours of daylight— running with the stars!

One fall there were two nights of Northern Lights that illuminated my way around the park. My daughter Eva had come along for one of those runs. When I stopped in utter awe, and started tearing up because it was so beautiful, she said with the characteristic disdain that children often have for their parent's emotions, "Oh Mom!"

When I look to the night skies, I not only feel close to God, I sense my father's presence. He's always there in every little star.

*****

As I run along here in Florida I see the moon rising. Every time I look up to the moon, I don't see some strange impersonal face. I see a very familiar and comforting visage, and I feel a pull. I was born to look up to that magnificent circle of light, the disc of luminosity, that ancient smile.

My dad believed we would go to the moon long before others even imagined it a possibility. I oftentimes imagine his reaction and excitement to that first landing, although it didn't happen until three and a half years after his death. But it was not meant to be.

Many a night, my father would bring out his telescope, get it carefully set up, and then give us turns looking out into the universe. In between the jostling around and trying to be the first to look we'd see such sights as Venus, sometimes in its crescent phase. We'd see four of the moons of Jupiter reaching out in a line on either side of the planet. The rings around Saturn always fascinated me. The planet looked so unreal, and yet, there it was—just like in the pictures! But here we were "soaking up" this light.

I love the fact that the light we see from the planets, the stars, and the moon becomes a part of us. It is absorbed into the eye, the energy seeping into us.

The moon was always my favorite. To get a good clear look at those craters and realize that it isn't a face (or rabbit) at all. The luminous landscape is a magical experience. Seeing it up close and personal changes you—maybe just a little bit, but it changes you nonetheless.

Daddy would even cart the telescope to the shore house and set it up out on the deck on those star-filled nights. I'll never forget the time he pointed out the Teapot constellation, and Scorpius, the winding creature hovering above the horizon with its tail reaching into the Milky Way. Scorpio, my astrological sign. I marveled at this star-studded region of the sky.

The July/August issue of *Ad Astra* magazine in 1991 listed my father as one of the 100 stars of space. The issue celebrated "the 100 space people who have had the greatest impact on our lives." There is the picture and article of my dad sharing the page with Alan B. Shepard, Jr., following the article touting Ronald Reagan's contributions to space development. The photo shows him sitting, reading with his wire-rimmed glasses. His thoughtful look as he peruses the astronautical paper in his hands is a pose I so often remember him in.

The article begins, "The future isn't what it used to be, because Dandridge Cole is no longer with us." How true. And those that lost him in the space program can never know to what depth he would be lost to his friends, his parents, siblings, wife and six children.

Since his death, I've always thought of my dad residing in the heavens, traveling faster than the speed of light, from one star to another, from planet to planet, then stopping briefly, taking a moment to smile down from the moon with his telescope pointed towards Earth.

*****

They hand out glow sticks to all of us competitors. Is this so we won't get lost? Or perhaps, like I said to the little child that ran out and asked me if he could have my stick, "No, I'm going to need this so they can find me when I pass out!"

The trail of gently bobbing lights that now line the course give a magical feel to it, like a path of stars or a milky way of lights ahead, bobbing on an astral sea.

I think of nights filled with lightening bugs when I was living in Philadelphia. The warm, humid nights were a perfect backdrop for these luminescent creatures of the dark. Ah, youth! I can still hear the giggles and see the wild, grabbing tiny hands trying to catch those bugs out of the air. We'd catch jars full of them and use them as lights.

In a boot camp letter, my father spoke of taping one of these phosphorescent bugs on his helmet. I smile thinking of the tough man trudging along in the dark with the spot of light on his head gear, and the little boy still hiding in that serviceman's soul.

Chapter Seven:
The Walk

"While the future holds great stress and threat as well as great challenges, we also see basis for expectations of the growth of man to a state of greater wisdom, greater accomplishment and greater happiness in the wonderful world beyond tomorrow."
—Dandridge M. Cole from **Beyond Tomorrow**

At the midway point, I come to the realization that if I keep running I probably won't finish, but if I walk, I'll finish.

Those first 13.2 miles I managed to average an eleven minute mile pace, and I felt like I was flying. In training, it was hard to run that slow, but today it seems to be as fast as I can manage. Biking 112 miles and swimming 2.4 does take it out of you!

My digestive system has certainly indicated this. I can't seem to stomach anything at this point. Even water or Gatorade are not sitting well with me. Waves of nausea come and go. And if this doesn't remind me of pregnancy! I inherited this wonderful cast-iron stomach when it comes to the 24 hour flu, never having a problem with it, no matter how many times

I've been exposed. So I naively thought that I'd have no problems with morning sickness. Boy! Was I wrong! About four weeks into my pregnancy with Norah, I was so sick morning, noon and night that I couldn't keep anything down. In those first three months I managed to lose ten pounds. Not something a ninety-pound pregnant woman should do. And the sickness didn't go away after the first three months. It just lessened enough that I was able to keep some food down.

I figure I made up for all those years of no stomach flu with the four years (or four ten month segments) of morning sickness. When I asked my mom about her experiences with morning sickness with her six pregnancies, she said it wasn't that bad, just the typical three month nausea.

It was later on, having a conversation with my Aunt Aubrey (my dad's sister) that I discovered who I was patterned after. She had been really sick the entire pregnancy with each of her children just as her mom had experienced the same. Who would've thought this was something passed on through my father. Thanks, Dad!

*****

About all I can handle is the little cups of ice they offer at the aid stations. They really have covered all the bases here. They have everything you need at these aid stations—food, drink, Bandaids, Vaseline (for the chafing), cold sponges, everything short of mints on the pillow!

My eye eventually stopped hurting but my lower left leg is starting to ache. Once again I have to ignore these minor inconveniences. It's not like I'd quit at this point. I've come too far to let go of this dream.

At the sixteen mile mark, I think back to a grueling sixteen mile training run that I'd done back on a cold winter morning. I remember feeling so satisfied and proud of myself for surviving it. I came home chilled and ready to jump into a hot tub of water.

I bathed then curled up into my bed to read more of the boot camp letters I had just gotten from my aunt and mom. I happened to pick up one that my father wrote of an eighteen mile training walk/run that they had done on a bivouac when he was in Alabama. In humid 115 degree temperatures with their full gear on these guys had to go eighteen miles! They were trying to "separate the men from the boys". My feelings of satisfaction and pride with my 16 mile run in the cold very quickly turned to humility.

Once again I'm awestruck at what we can do when we set our minds to it.

*****

I walk past a home with a white picket fence and flowers in the yard. Though it's now dark, the porch light shines on the flowers that are purple and rust colored. Were they mums? For years I hated chrysanthemums and I didn't even know why. But one fall day I brushed against a mum, releasing that acrid smell, and it dawned on me why I disliked them so much. They reminded me of that day, a day that has forever been etched in my mind and yet clouded over by the veil of denial.

There was nothing good about the day my dad died, nothing positive. It was Friday of the Halloween weekend; parties and talk of trick or treating occupied every kids mind at school. But instead of going home at lunchtime, as was our regular routine, my siblings and I went to the home of my sister's friend, Jeri. And after the quick afternoon school session we walked home. I don't think any of us had a clue as to what storm lay ahead, though Jeri has said she suspected Steve knew something wasn't quite right.

After dropping my stuff on the floor in that tired, just-got-home-from-school routine, I lay around reading Eerie magazine on my bed, goofing off after the long day of learning. Little did I know how eerie my world was about to become. I didn't even get up when I heard the car pull into the driveway, which meant my mom had returned. I'm sure there was a part of me that suspected something was not right, and by ignoring my mother's arrival I could delay or deny the inevitable.

I remember my sister Jency coming upstairs, and with tears in her eyes she relayed to me that Daddy was dead. I was so angry that she would try to trick me that way. I couldn't accept the reality of what she said. I ran downstairs to tell Mom what an awful joke Jency had pulled, but in the back of my throat I fought the dread rising up that it could be true. When I got to the bottom of the stairs, I knew. I knew the coldest, hardest truth any child could ever be given, as almost every person in the room was wiping tears or convulsing in sobs. It was at that moment I felt the switch click off. The light in my world had disappeared into a darkness I could never have imagined, and it would remain "off" for many, many years.

All of us children hovered around my mom like bees around their queen. But unlike the support those bees provide to the mother of the hive, we clung to her perhaps in an attempt to make sure she didn't also disappear. She sat there in that quiet, composed demeanor she so often displayed, and unlike everyone else in the room, she wore a stoic front with no tears. I thought she was so strong—too strong. My brother Stephen relates remembering she had walked in the door and, in shock or too numb to show emotion, simply stated that Daddy had died. Stephen took on a very heavy burden that day. Suddenly he was the man of the family and he accepted this role bravely.

My poor mom. She always hated being the center of attention. And here she was, thrust into the very center of it having the lead role in this tragic scene.

The days that followed were filled with a constant stream of people in and out. The noise of the ongoing chatter was just a drone in the background, barely cutting through the numbing wall around me.

The living room and dining room were filled with flower arrangements covering every surface. Even all the arrangements full of colorful blooms, many of them with potent-smelling chrysanthemums, couldn't cut through the pall. What normally would fill my heart with joy only served as a reminder that this was to be a milestone, a millstone hung around the tiny neck of a soon-to-be-eleven year old girl .

I could barely touch the meals that came in. Jeri's mother, who had so kindly cared for us Friday, cooked us meals and came over to do laundry and other chores in the days that followed. The whole time period surrounding the event hung like a dark cloud. But there was one little shaft of light that came through the cloud, and it came in the shape of eclairs.

Jeri's mom made us homemade eclairs. Perhaps she filled them with all the love and sympathy one could muster in the throes of such grief, because I had never tasted anything so comforting. It was the only thing that pierced through the impenetrable cloak that wrapped around me.

During those days in the fog, we tried to maintain some normalcy. But can one really just forge ahead like nothing has happened when your whole world has been thrown asunder?

We threw ourselves back into our routines too quickly. We went to our scheduled Halloween parties, but my friends couldn't comprehend how I felt. They didn't know what to say, so they said nothing or they avoided me. Most of the adults didn't seem to know what to say either. They would say things like wasn't it wonderful that Heaven needed him, or that he's gone "to a better place". A better place!? I still don't know how someone can say that to a child who just lost the lifeline to their existence!

Even in later years, my husband would ask why I still felt that grief. Why did I "hang on" to it.

It's like losing a leg. To lose a parent is like losing a body part. It's the leg that holds you up, takes you places, or runs from danger. It's the arm that pulls you up when you are down, cradles you, or shields you. It's the eyes that see all the beauty in life, or the dangers up ahead. It's the ears that hear symphonies in everyday things like birds singing or children laughing, or the warnings of sirens. It's the nose that takes in the fragrance, stirring the memory, or protecting you from the rancid smell of the things you shouldn't touch.

Sure, whatever piece of you that you lose, it heals over, but will there ever be a time where you don't miss that part of you? Those integral people in your life, those closest to you are part of your cellular makeup, without which you are no longer whole. Sure you heal. You move on. But there is always that "something" missing—a ghost limb of the soul.

*****

The ache in my leg is really bothering me (I'd find out later it was because the chip band became too tight) I'm retaining fluid, which is not a good sign. The silver ID bracelet they attached to my wrist at registration has now become uncomfortably tight, but once again, ignore, persevere!

Luckily, I am wearing no rings. My dad was cautious about wearing rings. He said wearing rings lowers your survival rate. I wasn't quite sure what he meant by that. But when you're an adventurer they just get in the way.

I never did like wearing rings. I stopped wearing my wedding band long before I divorced, due to a volleyball injury. I fractured the knuckle of that finger, and didn't wear the ring for months. After that, the ring just never felt comfortable on my finger again. I was always nervous about re-injuring the finger. Sometimes there are little signs like that foretelling the future.

*****

The days surrounding my dad's death were a blur. A group of us congregated at the house to head over to the cemetery including Aunt Katie, Uncle Richard, my Grandpa Cole and others. Aunt Katie has told me that moments before leaving Grandpa suddenly raised his hands and said, "He's in the room." This was not the Grandpa Cole I remembered. It seemed very out of character. He was the cerebral, non-emotional type. And as suddenly as he put up his hands, just as suddenly he lowered them and said "He's gone now." I like to think my dad was playing games with his tough old dad.

We went to the burial and funeral service that Sunday in October, a family of zombies, numb and drained. We walked down to the small wooded area of the Bryn Athyn Cemetery, a beautiful quiet, secluded spot down the hill from Cairncrest, a place normally alive with woodpeckers and other woodland birds. But I don't remember hearing any of the haunting, echoing trills of the wood thrush, that would have been so fitting in the setting, or the distant squawks of the ring-necked pheasant normally so prolific to the area. Perhaps I couldn't hear them because my head was so filled with the numbing shock.

My mom showed up at the interment with freshly washed hair, still wet, either not caring whether she might get sick, or more likely, not even realizing that she was there exposed to the cool fall air. I wonder now how we functioned at all.

My father was laid to rest next to his mother under a cluster of boxwood. My mind flashed back to times when I'd hidden among the boxwood at my Cole grandparents' home with my father hunting me down, saying "Now where did that little elf disappear to?" It was now the elf-catcher who disappeared into the boxwood.

I watched as my father's body was lowered into the ground, all the while wishing I could've seen his body. I didn't believe he could really be in that box. He was too alive a person to be dead! This just could not be. There was no reality in this moment.

You move along in a daze. You put one foot in front of the next not knowing how you will find the courage or strength to move forward.

How do we push ahead? It's at this point that something takes over, that invisible force, that imperceptible presence that gently takes our hand and leads us out of the dark place, or carries our weakened body out of the hole. It's that all-knowing, all-powerful force that comes from the beginning of all time.

*****

Baby steps. They may be little, but as long as they're still moving forward they'll get me to my destination. I think of a toddler's first steps.

This was something I watched with joy and celebration as each of my four children accomplished this feat (one as early as seven months!)

They take that first step totally unaware of the mountains they will have to climb. They take those steps instinctively, so crucial to our survival. And that first step towards any goal is always the biggest one.

I look up to the moon and can't help but be reminded of Neil Armstrong's momentous steps. "One small step for man, one giant leap for mankind."

Oh, if only my dad could have seen it.

And what a giant leap this was for me to take on this challenge—such tiny steps, and yet so huge.

I chant my mantra: "It's not how fast, or how far you go. It's about always moving forward."

Little steps, putting one foot in front of the other. Sometimes I'll count steps, strokes, or cadence, even breaths. Sometimes it's the only way to get through a tough period. It's meditative, and takes my mind off the pain. It's a great tool in the toolbox of life.

I start chatting with a woman who is in the same boat that I am, down to a walk, a stroll through the night air. There sure are a lot of us "strolling" along here! We talk about kids and life in general. And then I stop at a port-o-potty and lose my newly-made friend.

It amazes me, the variety of athletes reduced to walking.

There are the young, really fit looking athletes down to the types that make you wonder how they could possibly be doing this type of race at all. Old, young, male, female, thin and not so thin, even some of the elites—a real cross section of people all out on their "walkabout", their journey.

In endurance racing, "hitting the wall" or "bonking" is the condition caused by depleting the glycogen stores in the liver and muscles causing the fatigue and loss of energy. And just as hitting the wall can knock down an otherwise healthy athlete, so can tragedy, in an instant, yank the ground out from underneath you.

Tragedy knows no demographic. It strikes randomly, any place and anytime. It is a part of life.

Death is a part of life. We can deny it, but no one can escape it. It is one of the few things we can count on. Learning to accept it is part of the circle of life and valuing what you have and treasuring it, while at the same time realizing it is not yours to own—this is the lesson.

We have no control over our journey. We can train and prepare, but in the end we have no power over how it will play out. We can only control how we are affected by the journey.

To work towards the goal and learn from the journey leading up to it—this is the purpose—the end.

I walk for a time with a young guy in his early thirties. He has to be at least six feet tall, his long hair moist with sweat and topped with a bandana. He tells me his name just as the woman I last walked with did, but it's gone from my memory almost as quickly as he says it.

Names don't matter right now. We're in a state not unlike a drunken stupor, stumbling along (I think I'm slurring my speech) but all tied together in a chain of energy, a flow of determination. It's a good place to be near the end of a great day—a momentous day!

I stop again at another blue-green temple of excrement. Yes, at this point in my day, I'm spending more and more time sitting in the most disgusting looking chambers of horrors. And to spare the reader I will not get into any more of the gory details of these last few moments spent in the blue-green cubicles of hell! If I were to elaborate any more, it could put a fear so great into a potential competitor that I will refrain from any more discouragement.

And I will say, as I've said after every difficult labor I had with my children, " The pain and grueling conditions are certainly worth it all in the end!"

The last few miles are a blur. The determination I felt throughout the day is fading. Determination is replaced by a zombie-like trance. Perhaps knowing the end is near and that I can do it has lulled me into complacency.

The tank is dry. I'm going to just tip my head forward, putting it into auto pilot, and imagine there is a hill I'm going to coast down though it's as flat as a pancake here.

In the last quarter mile, in the darkness of night, a woman passes me, walking, whispering a weak "Good job."

I look down at her calf and there's a 46 written in weathered looking marker. She's in my age group! She's in my age group and I don't even have the strength to walk faster. With the weakest fist I've ever raised, I add "Go for it!"

I don't care about beating anyone at this point. This is my own battle that I must finish, that I must win. Winning for me is surviving. Winning for me is finishing in time to get the finisher's medal. And I'll make that goal by almost three hours.

Competition is a great motivator, but the best competing you can do is with yourself. I like to focus on beating my own personal bests, personal records, "P.R.'s".

Winning my age group category is a wonderful "high", but it's just the dessert at the end of a good meal. The good meal is the sustenance.

I won't win my age group here (and as it turned out, I didn't even come close!) But that's okay. It is a P.R. just to finish. And even if I ever do another Ironman, and finish faster, there is nothing that can top the first. There is something precious about a person's inaugural IM, something indescribable.

But my thoughts turn back to the reality I'm in, the sweaty, drained, stumbling reality I never could have pictured.

The cheers grow louder as I approach the finish.

I think of the inspiring music they play for the finish line segments of the Hawaii IM on TV, always beautiful and stirring, and always bringing the tears to my eyes. I don't have enough salt for tears at this point.

I start a feeble run. You have to run across the finish line! But it's like running when you have had a glass of wine too many.

I run down the chute lined with people cheering, yelling, but it's almost like a slow motion section of a movie clip where all the voices and faces just blur together. I'm thankful that they've "stuck it out" to this 9:00 hour to welcome us back.

I run to the finish line—the finish line...Whew! And there's never been a bigger "Whew!" as this one. THE FINISH LINE!

Chapter Eight:
The Finish

"It is difficult to say what is impossible. The dream of yesterday is the hope of today, and the reality of tomorrow."
—Dr Robert H. Goddard, The Father of American Rocketry

Finish lines are a beginning. And a finish line like this is a place of great magnitude, and unless you've crossed one you can't quite grasp the enormity of the moment. When you cross that line you pass through the realms of possibility. New paths open up into auspicious new worlds.

This Ironman race is the toughest physical and mental thing I've ever willingly done. But there's no question in my mind that I would rather do this race many times over than experience the devastating loss of my father again.

I come to the finish line and rip through the tape they put up for each athlete. Every one of us can enjoy a moment of glory as if we were the very first to cross. "Nenikekamen!" "We have won!"

Just like after all the long labors with each of my babies I am too tired to shed a tear of satisfaction. There is no strength left to raise my arms in a two fisted victory salute. But the change in me crossing that thin little line is so profound, as if I'm stepping into a Grand Canyon of change. The "me" before this line and the "me" after are two very different people.

When I started this adventure I set out with a goal in mind. In fact, it was three degrees of a goal. I would be HAPPY to finish by the seventeen hour cut-off. And then HAPPIER to finish around fourteen hours. And finally HAPPIEST if I could finish under thirteen hours. Well as it turned out I was happier than I could have imagined. I finished in 14hours, 10mins. And 49 seconds. I made it, but 600 athletes wouldn't.

Volunteers wrap me in the foil "space" blanket. A little part of me wanted to do the race just to get this special blanket. And the thing that makes it so special is that I've earned it. And not unlike those that travel into space, I feel like I've been to a different planet, to the moon. I've gone to the moon and back, finally standing here on the solid ground of earth.

My legs are wobbly, and the finisher's medal around my neck weighs me down. I have a new understanding of gravity, the strange and miraculous phenomenon it really is. It doesn't hit me. I can't really grasp what I've done. All I want to do is sit. I just want to stop and let the world catch up to me. A volunteer squats to take my chip band off my leg. She knows that to lean over or squat for us athletes is a move next to impossible.

I look down. With a tired head shaking shrug I realize that this band was the reason my leg was aching in that spot. It had dug into my skin when I swelled up, and I was left with a big bump and bruise. I'd become so out of it in these last few hours it didn't occur to me to stop and look to see why my leg hurt. You get to a point of just ignoring all the pain.

How can there be such satisfaction in a moment where

you are so completely spent, so completely drained. It's as if time has stopped, as if I've died in this instant and just as suddenly been reborn.

It's such a grand moment, so sublime, not unlike listening to a crescendo that builds throughout a good piece of music like Aaron Copeland's "Appalachian Spring," rising, growing, all the instruments building to this profoundly powerful peak and then gently slipping into the delicate, ever so soft strains of the strings. The quiet, the peace, the satisfaction wraps around you...

My sisters join me in the finishing area. The photographer wants to get my picture, but I am too weak to stand. He's very attentive and runs over to get some pretzels for me. The salt tastes so good now that my stomach has settled with the cessation of movement. I manage to stand and be photographed in a brief and glorious moment of fame in front of the flags. I smile as if it was a piece of cake to accomplish such a feat. But my poor body tells me differently, aching to just get back to the condo. It will be one of the most welcome nights of sleep I could ever imagine.

Somehow we manage to get back to the condo. I grab my gear from the transition area in my drunken stupor and shakily transport my bike to the car, using it as my "walker" with Jency and Cathy on either side. We load the bike into the trunk, my trusty blue friend who I now have a very different relationship with. I picture leaning over to plant a big kiss on the cold metal frame, but worry that any such action could be my last for the night, I need to reserve what little strength I have to get to my destination. I fall into the back seat, thinking that bed cannot come too soon.

Back at the condo I somehow manage to get cleaned up.

There is no greater "clean" than the clean of showering or bathing away the sweat and salt of a day like this. There is an entitlement to this kind of clean, a ritual or ceremony not to be taken lightly—a baptism.

I remember moments after long training runs or rides where I'd actually drift off into a brief but contented snooze while still nestled in my tub. But I hold off till I climb into the welcoming arms of bed. I don't know that a bed has ever felt so good.

Finally I'm curled up in my bed in a fetal position awaiting the blessed submission of sleep and I drift into the depth of where I've been this day. I've traveled to a land where maybe only three percent of the population may ever visit.

I lie there, my mind wandering around in that land of Euphoria. It's a land of adventure where stories abound, stories almost myth-like in their unbelievable feats of strength and battles of will. It's a place where anything is possible, and I hear the haunting voice of my dad, that pillar of my life. The gentle yet strong timbre of his words come back to me saying, "Anything is possible. Anything you want badly enough, and are willing to work for, you can have."

He was right!

And like some Brocken Spectre, those ethereal apparitions that appear in a foggy setting, those prism-surrounded ghosts that so often turn out to be just a reflection of yourself, Daddy comes into my life and then disappears. He's the shadow I see behind me, following me in the light but hiding in those dark moments, waiting for me to call on him.

Our destiny is to awaken from our spiritual amnesia, to open our eyes to our world and really see it with the clear-sightedness of a hawk.

In Native American culture, the hawk represents a messenger. It's spirit appears in our life when we need to pay attention to the subtle messages around us. There have been so many messages, right there in front of my face. But so often over the years I was too numb, too asleep to see them.

I've started paying attention.

How prophetic the title of a science fiction novel was that Dad wrote in 1953, **The Reaper Came Too Soon**, as was the book he enjoyed when he was in his twenties, **Life Is Too Short** by C. Kay-Scott. His life ended all too soon. Here was a person so full of life, and so conscientious of living actively.

Just as my grandfather said when putting on a red bow tie instead of the traditional black for my grandmother's funeral service, "You can't kill a spirit." He knew she would've preferred the colorful red tie. Like my grandmother's, my father's spirit didn't die.

You can't destroy energy, that energy we are all a part of. The light from the moon, the twinkling stars, and the planets become part of us, and the sun's warm energy soaks into us. That force doesn't ever disappear. It stays a part of us.

We tap into that flow of energy every time we exercise, every time we step out into nature. We tap into it through meditation, sleep, and eating healthily. We soak it up with every positive connection we have with people, with every good intention and action.

No, my father's spirit will never die. It lives on in his ideas, his visions, his books, poems, songs, and words of wisdom. It lives on through his children, grandchildren, and great grandchildren, and will continue to spill through the generations forever.

As a child I was taught we are supposed to look to our

God and the Church as our father and mother. As I've grown into an adult, I've transferred this recognition to owners that seem more right to me.

My God, my father, is that source of energy, the origin of all possibility. My Church, my mother, is the great outdoors, those open arms held out in welcome, free of condemnation and criticism.

Perhaps I held my father up on a pedestal too long, stuck in an eleven-year-old's idea of who he was. But this journey has lead me on a path of discovery. I think of that canoe, that big red canoe named Discovery, and I think of all I learned from this man. In this search, things I'd forgotten have all but risen again.

He was a man of iron, but even ironmen fall. They fall, and then they rise again, out of the fog of denied existence, from avoidance of pain, into the halls of remembrance. They rise to be forever immortalized in pictures and words.

As I drift off into sleep, I hear the loud voice of the announcer, Mike Reilly (the legendary voice of Ironman) still ringing in my head "You ARE an Ironman!"

Afterthought:
Stream of
Providence

Stream of Providence

In every mountain that we move
In every step that we improve
There is a current pulling us along
Washing away our weakness
To make us strong
In every flower that we grow
In every truth there is to know
In every moment that is ours to use
Underlying currents there Allow us to choose
Deep flows the Stream of Providence
Warm and alive
Within that Stream of Providence
Our spirits thrive
Upon that Stream of Providence
Floating we live
Ever flows that Stream of Providence
Our every breath it gives
In every love we have to share
In every loss we have to bear
There is that stream that will forever run
There to wade into for everyone
—Martha Cole Childs (1987)

151

*****

Ironman changed my life in a way I never could have dreamed. In retrospect, I see it as one of the greater dividing lines in my life.

A few months after my race I was training with a friend, someone who had done other ironman races. I was confiding in her that I'd never gotten a college degree, and felt that doing Ironman was like getting that longed-for accolade. She said, "Oh, Martha, I not only have a college degree, but a Master's, and what Ironman has done for me goes well beyond what any degree has done."

Ironman has made me a better person, more confident, more positive, and more creative, though that is not something I would have foreseen. It has taken my life in a direction toward peace and happiness.

After over a hundred pages here, I still feel like I can't begin to describe how grateful I am that I found this new avenue to run, or to walk! I used to be a sedentary person, and when I just sit the energy drains from my body, my pulse slows, I get listless and tired. Moving, just walking around the neighborhood or even doing breathing exercises re-energizes me and fills me with life.

I worry about the sedentary lifestyle Americans seem to embrace—too much sitting in front of a TV or computer. We're turning into a lifeless society. More people should be like Norton Davies, the 82-year old that did the Ironman that year. I heard after the race that he hadn't finished by the 17th hour mark to get the finisher's medal. But he finished and the race director had gone out and finished the last hour with him.

I've had some call my lifestyle a hobby and have even

been accused of it being selfish or indulgent. I wonder about people who state these things. They don't see that it has increased my output tremendously. I am twice the person I was before, and I will continue swimming, running, or biking until I die. I don't want to just exist. I want to live, and enjoy living, and to have that high quality of life.

Some people look towards another life, Heaven as their goal, spending life on this planet waiting to get to "the other side" where perhaps the grass is greener. But I firmly believe you have to find your "Heaven" here, wherever you are. You have to find it in each moment, in every activity, in every direction you turn. If you can't find it here, you won't find it there either.

As tremendous an impact as this race had on my life, I realize it was just another step toward finding peace, getting me to this point where I've rediscovered a person I thought I had lost. Now that I've written this story, it's as if I got that leg back, that body part I lost when I lost my dad. I have him back in a way I never could've imagined, recorded now, so nothing will be forgotten.

There is a current, a "flow," that can fill our life with rewards—a fulfillment if we choose to enter it. If you allow it, it can do most of the work for you. The physical body may put out the effort, but if you can trust in this flux, this force of energy, your mind can relax and enjoy the journey.

And for those of you who think you can't do something of this magnitude, know that you can. You can do whatever it is you set out to do if you have enough determination, and enough trust. If you want it badly enough and are willing to work for it, you can do it! It may not be the way anyone else does it, but YOU CAN DO IT. You may not be as fast, or go as far as someone else. But nothing holds you back except the idea that you can't!

It's not about how fast or how far you go. It's about always moving FORWARD—moving forward within the flow.

Acknowledgements

Writing is easy. Getting this book polished up to present it to the public is another story. I would like to thank all the many people that were a part of this process. I am ever so grateful for all the work put into this project by such loving hands and hearts.

Thank you to my Aunt Aubrey Odhner and big brother Stephen Cole for the wealth of information they contributed and a big thank you to Amanda Childs, Andy Bruce and Aunt Katie Goerwitz for their editing and support.

I want to thank all those athletes who were instrumental in my training: Ken V., Ray D., Deb C. And thanks to all those athletes that continue to inspire me: Jim L., Scott D., Bill O., King and June Y. and Wayne Z.

I'm grateful to those friends particularly David and Jenny C., Gail G., Mandy S., Jayne B., Renne K., Jim Mc., Dave K., Thomas N., and my children (Norah Eva, Amanda and Adam), my siblings and mom who stood by me and believed in me. And even a thank you for all those friends and family members who didn't. It's always good to have a healthy dose of people doubting you. It inspires you to show them differently!

A big thank you goes out to Iris Lee Underwood for encouraging me, teaching me and inspiring me to pursue this project. And thanks to Roy Scarfo, Chris Clark, Russell Craig, Kevin Hanson, Bill Rodgers and Joe Morton for your positive words and feedback on this project.

A special thank you goes out to Joe Morton and XanGo. Joe has contributed so much to the health of so many. And XanGo is a big reason why I am able to continue doing what I love—running, swimming, biking and BREATHING!

A huge thank you to Sherry McLaughlin for her amazing energy putting this together. Another huge thank you to Jon and Karin Childs for doing the work to finish up this project and get it into print.

And last, but not least, a special thank you to my mother, the woman who picked up all the shattered pieces of our young lives and carefully held them together through all these years and to my dad who, though his physical presence is gone, still inspires me.

And finally, to the energy behind all of this—the voice that started as a whisper and grew to an encouraging yell, the Creator of all things possible.